DELICIOUS BAKE RECIPES 2021

FLAVORFUL RECIPES EASY TO MAKE FOR BEGINNERS (INCLUDES BREAD AND CROISSANT RECIPES)

STEPHANIE PEARSON

Table of Contents

Bavarian Rye Bread

Makes two 450 g/1 lb loaves

For the sourdough:

150 g/5 oz/1¼ cups rye flour

5 ml/1 tsp dried yeast

150 ml/¼ pt/2/3 cup warm water

For the loaf:

550 g/1¼ lb/5 cups wholemeal (wholewheat) flour

50 g/2 oz/½ cup rye flour

5 ml/1 tsp salt

25 g/1 oz fresh yeast or 40 ml/ 2½ tbsp dried yeast

350 ml/12 fl oz/1½ cups warm water

30 ml/2 tbsp caraway seeds

A little flour mixed to a paste with water

To make the sourdough, mix the rye flour, yeast and water until clear. Cover and leave overnight.

To make the loaf, mix together the flours and salt. Mix the yeast with the warm water and add to the flours with the sourdough. Stir in half the caraway seeds and mix to a dough. Knead well until elastic and no longer sticky. Place in an oiled bowl, cover with oiled clingfilm (plastic wrap) and leave in a warm place for about 30 minutes until doubled in size.

Knead again, shape into two 450 g/ 1 lb loaves and place on a greased baking (cookie) sheet. Brush with the flour and water paste and sprinkle with the remaining caraway seeds. Cover with oiled clingfilm and leave to rise for 30 minutes.

Bake in a preheated oven at 230°C/ 450°F/gas mark 8 for 30 minutes until dark golden and hollow-sounding when tapped on the base.

Light Rye Bread

Makes one 675 g/1½ lb loaf

15 g/½ oz fresh yeast or 20 ml/ 4 tsp dried yeast

5 ml/1 tsp caster (superfine) sugar

150 ml/¼ pt/2/3 cup warm water

225 g/8 oz/2 cups rye flour

400 g/14 oz/3½ cups strong plain (bread) flour

10 ml/2 tsp salt

300 ml/½ pt/1¼ cups warm milk

1 egg yolk, beaten

5 ml/1 tsp poppy seeds

Blend the yeast with the sugar and water and leave in a warm place until frothy. Mix together the flours and salt and make a well in the centre. Stir in the milk and yeast mixture and mix to a firm dough. Knead on a lightly floured surface until smooth and elastic. Place in an oiled bowl, cover with oiled clingfilm (plastic wrap) and leave in a warm place for about 1 hour until doubled in size.

Knead again lightly, then shape into a long loaf and place on a greased baking (cookie) sheet. Cover with oiled clingfilm and leave to rise for 30 minutes.

Brush with egg yolk and sprinkle with poppy seeds. Bake in a preheated oven at 200°C/400°F/gas mark 6 for 20 minutes. Reduce the oven temperature to 190°C/ 375°F/gas mark 5 and bake for a further 15 minutes until the bread is hollow-sounding when tapped on the base.

Rye Bread with Wheatgerm

Makes one 450 g/1 lb loaf

15 g/½ oz fresh yeast or 20 ml/ 4 tsp dried yeast

5 ml/1 tsp sugar

450 ml/¾ pt/2 cups warm water

350 g/12 oz/3 cups rye flour

225 g/8 oz/2 cups plain (all-purpose) flour

50 g/2 oz/½ cup wheatgerm

10 ml/2 tsp salt

45 ml/3 tbsp black treacle (molasses)

15 ml/1 tbsp oil

Blend the yeast with the sugar and a little of the warm water, then leave in a warm place until frothy. Mix together the flours, wheatgerm and salt and make a well in the centre. Blend in the yeast mixture with the treacle and oil and mix to a soft dough. Turn out on to a floured surface and knead for 10 minutes until smooth and elastic, or process in a food processor. Place in a oiled bowl, cover with oiled clingfilm (plastic wrap) and leave in a warm place for about 1 hour until doubled in size.

Knead again, then shape into a loaf and place on a greased baking (cookie) sheet. Cover with oiled clingfilm and leave to rise until doubled in size.

Bake in a preheated oven at 220°C/ 425°F/gas mark 7 for 15 minutes. Reduce the oven temperature to 190°C/375°F/gas mark 5 and bake for a further 40 minutes until the loaf sounds hollow when tapped on the base.

Sally Lunn

Makes two 450 g/1 lb loaves

500 ml/16 fl oz/2 cups milk

25 g/1 oz/2 tbsp butter or margarine

30 ml/2 tbsp caster (superfine) sugar

10 ml/2 tsp salt

20 ml/4 tsp dried yeast

60 ml/4 tbsp warm water

900 g/2 lb/8 cups strong plain (bread) flour

3 eggs, beaten

Bring the milk almost to a simmer, then add the butter or margarine, sugar and salt and stir well. Leave to cool until lukewarm. Dissolve the yeast in the warm water. Place the flour in a large bowl and mix in the milk, yeast and eggs. Mix to a soft dough and knead until elastic and no longer sticky. Cover with oiled clingfilm (plastic wrap) and leave to rise for 30 minutes.

Knead the dough again, then cover and leave to rise. Knead it a third time, then cover and leave to rise.

Shape the dough and place in two greased 450 g/1 lb loaf tins (pans). Cover and leave to rise until doubled in bulk. Bake in a preheated oven at 190°C/ 375°F/gas mark 5 for 45 minutes until golden on top and the loaves sound hollow when tapped on the base.

Samos Bread

Makes three 450 g/1 lb loaves

15 g/½ oz fresh yeast or 20 ml/ 4 tsp dried yeast

15 ml/1 tbsp malt extract

600 ml/1 pt/2½ cups warm water

25 g/1 oz/2 tbsp vegetable fat (shortening)

900 g/2 lb/8 cups wholemeal (wholewheat) flour

30 ml/2 tbsp milk powder (non-fat dry milk)

10 ml/2 tsp salt

15 ml/1 tbsp clear honey

50 g/2 oz/½ cup sesame seeds, roasted

25 g/1 oz/¼ cup sunflower seeds, roasted

Blend the yeast with the malt extract and a little of the warm water and leave in a warm place for 10 minutes until frothy. Rub the fat into the flour and milk powder, then stir in the salt and make a well in the centre. Pour in the yeast mixture, the remaining warm water and the honey and mix to a dough. Knead well until smooth and elastic. Add the seeds and knead for a further 5 minutes until well blended. Shape into three 450 g/1 lb loaves and place on a greased baking (cookie) sheet. Cover with oiled clingfilm (plastic wrap) and leave in a warm place for 40 minutes until doubled in size.

Bake in a preheated oven at 230°F/ 450°F/gas mark 8 for 30 minutes until golden brown and hollow-sounding when tapped on the base.

Sesame Baps

Makes 12

25 g/1 oz fresh yeast or 40 ml/ 2½ tbsp dried yeast

5 ml/1 tsp caster (superfine) sugar

150 ml/¼ pt/2/3 cup warm milk

450 g/1 lb/4 cups strong plain (bread) flour

5 ml/1 tsp salt

25 g/1 oz/2 tbsp lard (shortening)

150 ml/¼ pt/2/3 cup warm water

30 ml/2 tbsp sesame seeds

Blend the yeast with the sugar and a little of the warm milk and leave in a warm place until frothy. Mix the flour and salt in a bowl, rub in the lard and make a well in the centre. Pour in the yeast mixture, the remaining milk and the water and mix to a soft dough. Turn out on to a floured surface and knead for 10 minutes until smooth and elastic, or process in a food processor. Place in an oiled bowl, cover with oiled clingfilm (plastic wrap) and leave in a warm place for about 1 hour until doubled in size.

Knead again and shape into 12 rolls, flatten them slightly and arrange on a greased baking (cookie) sheet. Cover with oiled clingfilm (plastic wrap) and leave to rise in a warm place for 20 minutes.

Brush with water, sprinkle with seeds and bake in a preheated oven at 220°C/425°F/gas mark 7 for 15 minutes until golden.

Sourdough Starter

Makes about 450 g/1 lb

450 ml/¾ pt/2 cups lukewarm water

25 g/1 oz fresh yeast or 40 ml/ 2½ tbsp dried yeast

225 g/8 oz/2 cups plain (all-purpose) flour

2.5 ml/½ tsp salt

To feed:

225 g/8 oz/2 cups plain (all-purpose) flour

450 ml/¾ pt/2 cups lukewarm water

Mix together the main ingredients in a bowl, cover with muslin (cheesecloth) and leave in a warm place for 24 hours. Add 50 g/2 oz/½ cup plain flour and 120 ml/4 fl oz/½ cup lukewarm water, cover and leave for a further 24 hours. Repeat three times, by which time the mixture should smell sour, then transfer to the fridge. Replace any starter you use with an equal mixture of lukewarm water and flour.

Soda Bread

Makes one 20 cm/8 in loaf

450 g/1 lb/4 cups plain (all-purpose) flour

10 ml/2 tsp bicarbonate of soda (baking soda)

10 ml/2 tsp cream of tartar

5 ml/1 tsp salt

25 g/1 oz/2 tbsp lard (shortening)

5 ml/1 tsp caster (superfine) sugar

15 ml/1 tbsp lemon juice

300 ml/½ pt/1¼ cups milk

Mix together the flour, bicarbonate of soda, cream of tartar and salt. Rub in the lard until the mixture resembles breadcrumbs. Stir in the sugar. Mix the lemon juice into the milk, then stir it into the dry ingredients until you have a soft dough. Knead lightly, then shape the dough into a 20 cm/8 in round and flatten it slightly. Place it on a floured baking tray and mark into quarters with the blade of a knife. Bake in a preheated oven at 200°C/400°F/gas mark 6 for about 30 minutes until crusty on top. Leave to cool before serving.

Sourdough Bread

Makes two 350 g/12 oz loaves

250 ml/8 fl oz/1 cup lukewarm water

15 ml/1 tbsp caster (superfine) sugar

30 ml/2 tbsp melted butter or margarine

15 ml/1 tbsp salt

250 ml/8 fl oz/1 cup Sourdough Starter

2.5 ml/½ tsp bicarbonate of soda (baking soda)

450 g/1 lb/4 cups plain (all-purpose) flour

Mix together the water, sugar, butter or margarine and salt. Mix the sourdough starter with the bicarbonate of soda and stir into the mixture, then beat in the flour to make a stiff dough. Knead the dough until smooth and satiny, adding a little more flour if necessary. Place in an oiled bowl, cover with oiled clingfilm (plastic wrap) and leave in a warm place for about 1 hour until doubled in size.

Knead again lightly and shape into two loaves. Place on a greased baking (cookie) sheet, cover with oiled clingfilm and leave to rise for about 40 minutes until doubled in size.

Bake in a preheated oven at 190°C/ 375°F/gas mark 5 for about 40 minutes until golden brown and hollow-sounding when tapped on the base.

Sourdough Buns

Makes 12

50 g/2 oz/¼ cup butter or margarine

175 g/6 oz/1½ cups plain (all-purpose) flour

5 ml/1 tsp salt

2.5 ml/½ tsp bicarbonate of soda (baking soda)

250 ml/8 fl oz/1 cup Sourdough Starter

A little melted butter or margarine for glazing

Rub the butter or margarine into the flour and salt until the mixture resembles breadcrumbs. Mix the bicarbonate of soda into the starter, then stir it into the flour to make a stiff dough. Knead until smooth and no longer sticky. Shape into small rolls and arrange well apart on a greased baking (cookie) sheet. Brush the tops with butter or margarine, cover with oiled clingfilm (plastic wrap) and leave to rise for about 1 hour until doubled in size. Bake in a preheated oven at 220°C/425°F/gas mark 8 for 15 minutes until golden brown.

Vienna Loaf

Makes one 675 g/1½ lb loaf

15 g/½ oz fresh yeast or 20 ml/ 4 tsp dried yeast

5 ml/1 tsp caster (superfine) sugar

300 ml/½ pt/1¼ cups warm milk

40 g/1½ oz/3 tbsp butter or margarine

450 g/1 lb/4 cups strong plain (bread) flour

5 ml/1 tsp salt

1 egg, well beaten

Blend the yeast with the sugar and a little of the warm milk and leave in a warm place until frothy. Melt the butter or margarine and add the remaining milk. Blend together the yeast mixture, butter mixture, flour, salt and egg to make a soft dough. Knead until smooth and no longer sticky. Place in an oiled bowl, cover with oiled clingfilm (plastic wrap) and leave in a warm place for about 1 hour until doubled in size.

Knead the dough again, then shape into a loaf and place on a greased baking (cookie) sheet. Cover with oiled clingfilm and leave to rise in a warm place for 20 minutes.

Bake in a preheated oven at 230°C/ 450°F/gas mark 8 for 25 minutes until golden and hollow-sounding when tapped on the base.

Wholemeal Bread

Makes two 450 g/1 lb loaves

15 g/½ oz fresh yeast or 20 ml/ 4 tsp dried yeast

5 ml/1 tsp sugar

300 ml/½ pt/1¼ cups warm water

550 g/1¼ lb/5 cups wholemeal (wholewheat) flour

5 ml/1 tsp salt

45 ml/3 tbsp buttermilk

Sesame or caraway seeds for sprinkling (optional)

Blend the yeast with the sugar and a little of the warm water and leave in a warm place for 20 minutes until frothy. Place the flour and salt in a bowl and make a well in the centre. Stir in the yeast, the remaining water and the buttermilk. Work to a firm dough which leaves the sides of the bowl cleanly, adding a little extra flour or water if necessary. Knead on a lightly floured surface or in a processor until elastic and no longer sticky. Shape the dough into two greased 450 g/1 lb loaf tins (pans), cover with oiled clingfilm (plastic wrap) and leave to rise for about 45 minutes until the dough has risen just above the top of the tins.

Sprinkle with sesame or caraway seeds, if using. Bake in a preheated oven at 230°C/450°F/gas mark 8 for 15 minutes, then reduce the oven temperature to 190°C/375°F/gas mark 5 and bake for a further 25 minutes until golden brown and hollow-sounding when tapped on the base.

Wholemeal Honey Bread

Makes one 900 g/2 lb loaf

15 g/½ oz fresh yeast or 20 ml/ 4 tsp dried yeast

450 ml/¾ pt/2 cups warm water

45 ml/3 tbsp set honey

50 g/2 oz/¼ cup butter or margarine

750 g/1½ lb/6 cups wholemeal (wholewheat) flour

2.5 ml/½ tsp salt

15 ml/1 tbsp sesame seeds

Blend the yeast with a little of the water and a little of the honey and leave in a warm place for 20 minutes until frothy. Rub the butter or margarine into the flour and salt, then mix in the yeast mixture and the remaining water and honey until you have a soft dough. Knead until elastic and no longer sticky. Place in an oiled bowl, cover with oiled clingfilm (plastic wrap) and leave in a warm place for about 1 hour until doubled in size.

Knead again and shape into a greased 900 g/2 lb loaf tin (pan). Cover with oiled clingfilm and leave to rise for 20 minutes until the dough comes above the top of the tin.

Bake in a preheated oven at 220°C/ 425°F/gas mark 7 for 15 minutes. Reduce the oven temperature to 190°C/375°F/gas mark 5 and bake for a further 20 minutes until the loaf is golden brown and hollow-sounding when tapped on the base.

Quick Wholemeal Rolls

Makes 12

20 ml/4 tsp dried yeast

375 ml/13 fl oz/1½ cups warm water

50 g/2 oz/¼ cup soft brown sugar

100 g/4 oz/1 cup wholemeal (wholewheat) flour

100 g/4 oz/1 cup plain (all-purpose) flour

5 ml/1 tsp salt

Blend the yeast with the water and a little sugar and leave in a warm place until frothy. Stir into the flours and salt with the remaining sugar and mix to a soft dough. Spoon the dough into muffin tins (pans) and leave to rise for 20 minutes until the dough has risen to the top of the tins.

Bake in a preheated oven at 180°C/ 350°F/gas mark 4 for 30 minutes until well risen and golden brown.

Wholemeal Bread with Walnuts

Makes one 900 g/2 lb loaf

15 g/½ oz fresh yeast or 20 ml/ 4 tsp dried yeast

5 ml/1 tsp soft brown sugar

450 ml/¾ pt/2 cups warm water

450 g/1 lb/4 cups wholemeal (wholewheat) flour

175 g/6 oz/1½ cups strong plain (bread) flour

5 ml/1 tsp salt

15 ml/1 tbsp walnut oil

100 g/4 oz/1 cup walnuts, coarsely chopped

Blend the yeast with the sugar and a little of the warm water and leave in a warm place for 20 minutes until frothy. Mix the flours and salt in a bowl, add the yeast mixture, the oil and the remaining warm water and mix to a firm dough. Knead until smooth and no longer sticky. Place in an oiled bowl, cover with oiled clingfilm (plastic wrap) and leave in a warm place for about 1 hour until doubled in size.

Knead again lightly and work in the nuts, then shape into a greased 900 g/2 lb loaf tin (pan), cover with oiled clingfilm and leave in a warm place for 30 minutes until the dough has risen above the top of the tin.

Bake in a preheated oven at 220°C/ 425°F/gas mark 7 for 30 minutes until golden brown and hollow-sounding when tapped on the base.

Almond Plait

Makes one 450 g/1 lb loaf

15 g/½ oz fresh yeast or 20 ml/ 4 tsp dried yeast

40 g/1½ oz/3 tbsp caster (superfine) sugar

100 ml/3½ fl oz/6½ tbsp warm milk

350 g/12 oz/3 cups strong plain (bread) flour

2.5 ml/½ tsp salt

50 g/2 oz/¼ cup butter or margarine, melted

1 egg

For the filling and glaze:

50 g/2 oz Almond Paste

45 ml/3 tbsp apricot jam (conserve)

50g /2 oz/1/3 cup raisins

50 g/2 oz/½ cup chopped almonds

1 egg yolk

Blend the yeast with 5 ml/1 tsp of the sugar and a little of the milk and leave in a warm place for 20 minutes until frothy. Mix the flour and salt in a bowl and make a well in the centre. Mix in the yeast mixture, the remaining sugar and milk, the melted butter or margarine and the egg and mix to a smooth dough. Knead until elastic and no longer sticky. Place in an oiled bowl, cover with oiled clingfilm (plastic wrap) and leave in a warm place for about 1 hour until doubled in size.

Roll out the dough on a lightly floured surface to a 30 x 40 cm/12 x 16 in rectangle. Mix together the filling ingredients except the egg yolk and work until smooth, then spread down the centre one-third of the dough. Cut slashes in the outside two-thirds of the dough from the edges at an angle towards the filling at about 2 cm/¾ in intervals. Fold alternate left and right strips over the filling and seal the ends together firmly. Place on a greased baking (cookie) sheet, cover and leave in a warm place for 30 minutes until doubled in size. Brush with egg yolk and bake in a preheated oven at 190°C/375°F/gas mark 5 for 30 minutes until golden brown.

Brioches

Makes 12

15 g/½ oz fresh yeast or 20 ml/ 4 tsp dried yeast

30 ml/2 tbsp warm water

2 eggs, lightly beaten

225 g/8 oz/2 cups strong plain (bread) flour

15 ml/1 tbsp caster (superfine) sugar

2.5 ml/½ tsp salt

50 g/2 oz/¼ cup butter or margarine, melted

Mix together the yeast, water and eggs, then stir into the flour, sugar, salt and butter or margarine and mix to a soft dough. Knead until elastic and no longer sticky. Place in an oiled bowl, cover and leave in a warm place for about 1 hour until doubled in size.

Knead again, divide into 12 pieces, then break a small ball off each piece. Shape the larger pieces into balls and place in 7.5 cm/ 3 in fluted brioche or muffin tins (pans). Press a finger right through the dough, then press the remaining balls of dough on the top. Cover and leave in a warm place for about 30 minutes until the dough has reached just above the tops of the tins.

Bake in a preheated oven at 230°C/ 450°F/gas mark 8 for 10 minutes until golden.

Plaited Brioche

Makes one 675 g/1½ lb loaf

25 g/1 oz fresh yeast or 40 ml/ 2½ tbsp dried yeast

5 ml/1 tsp caster (superfine) sugar

250 ml/8 fl oz/1 cup warm milk

675 g/1½ lb/6 cups strong plain (bread) flour

5 ml/1 tsp salt

1 egg, beaten

150 ml/¼ pt/2/3 cup warm water

1 egg yolk

Blend the yeast with the sugar with a little of the warm milk and leave in a warm place for 20 minutes until frothy. Mix the flour and salt and make a well in the centre. Add the egg, the yeast mixture, the remaining warm milk and enough of the warm water to mix to a soft dough. Knead until soft and no longer sticky. Place in an oiled bowl, cover with oiled clingfilm (plastic wrap) and leave in a warm place for about 1 hour until doubled in size.

Knead the dough lightly, then divide into quarters. Roll three pieces into thin strips about 38 cm/15 in long. Moisten one end of each strip and press them together, then plait the strips together, moisten and fasten the ends. Place on a greased baking (cookie) sheet. Divide the remaining piece of dough into three, roll out into 38 cm/15 in strips and plait together in the same way to make a thinner plait. Beat the egg yolk with 15 ml/1 tbsp of water and brush over the large plait. Gently press the smaller plait on top and brush with the egg glaze. Cover and leave in a warm place to rise for 40 minutes.

Bake in a preheated oven at 200°C/ 400°F/gas mark 6 for 45 minutes until golden brown and hollow-sounding when tapped on the base.

Apple Brioches

Makes 12

For the dough:

15 g/½ oz fresh yeast or 10 ml/ 2 tsp dried yeast

75 ml/5 tbsp warm milk

100 g/4 oz/1 cup wholemeal (wholewheat) flour

350 g/12 oz/3 cups strong plain (bread) flour

30 ml/2 tbsp clear honey

4 eggs

A pinch of salt

200 g/7 oz/scant 1 cup butter or margarine, melted

For the filling:

75 g/3 oz apple purée (sauce)

25 g/1 oz/¼ cup wholemeal (wholewheat) breadcrumbs

25 g/3 oz/½ cup sultanas (golden raisins)

2.5 ml/½ tsp ground cinnamon

1 egg, beaten

To make the dough, blend the yeast with the warm milk and wholemeal flour and leave in a warm place for 20 minutes to ferment. Add the plain flour, honey, eggs and salt and knead well. Pour on the melted butter or margarine and continue to knead until the dough is elastic and smooth. Place in an oiled bowl, cover with oiled clingfilm (plastic wrap) and leave in a warm place for about 1 hour until doubled in size.

Mix together all the filling ingredients except the egg. Shape the dough into 12 pieces, then take one-third off each piece. Shape the larger pieces to fit greased fluted brioche or muffin tins (pans). Press a large hole almost through to the base with a finger or fork handle and fill with the filling. Shape each of the smaller dough pieces into a ball, moisten the top of the dough and press over the filling to seal it into the brioche. Cover and leave in a warm place for 40 minutes until almost doubled in size.

Brush with beaten egg and bake in a preheated oven at 220°C/425°F/gas mark 7 for 15 minutes until golden.

Tofu and Nut Brioches

Makes 12

For the dough:

15 g/½ oz fresh yeast or 20 ml/ 4 tsp dried yeast

75 ml/5 tbsp warm milk

100 g/4 oz/1 cup wholemeal (wholewheat) flour

350 g/12 oz/3 cups strong plain (bread) flour

30 ml/2 tsp clear honey

4 eggs

A pinch of salt

200 g/7 oz/scant 1 cup butter or margarine, melted

For the filling:

50 g/2 oz/¼ cup tofu, diced

25 g/1 oz/¼ cup cashew nuts, toasted and chopped

25 g/1 oz chopped mixed vegetables

½ onion, chopped

1 garlic clove, chopped

2.5 ml/½ tsp dried mixed herbs

2.5 ml/½ tsp French mustard

1 egg, beaten

To make the dough, blend the yeast with the warm milk and wholemeal flour and leave in a warm place for 20 minutes to ferment. Add the plain flour, honey, eggs and salt and knead well. Pour on the melted butter or margarine and continue to knead until the dough is elastic and smooth. Place in an oiled bowl, cover with oiled clingfilm (plastic wrap) and leave in a warm place for about 1 hour until doubled in size.

Mix together all the filling ingredients except the egg. Shape the dough into 12 pieces, then take one-third off each piece. Shape the larger pieces to fit greased fluted brioche or muffin tins (pans). Press a large hole almost through to the base with a finger or fork handle and fill with the filling. Shape each of the smaller dough pieces into a ball, moisten the top of the dough and press over the filling to seal it into the brioche. Cover and leave in a warm place for 40 minutes until almost doubled in size.

Brush with beaten egg and bake in a preheated oven at 220°C/425°F/gas mark 7 for 15 minutes until golden.

Chelsea Buns

Makes 9

225 g/8 oz/2 cups strong plain (bread) flour

5 ml/1 tsp caster (superfine) sugar

15 g/½ oz fresh yeast or 20 ml/ 4 tsp dried yeast

120 ml/4 fl oz/½ cup warm milk

A pinch of salt

15 g/½ oz/1 tbsp butter or margarine

1 egg, beaten

For the filling:
75 g/3 oz/½ cup mixed dried fruit (fruit cake mix)

25 g/1 oz/3 tbsp chopped mixed (candied) peel

50 g/2 oz/¼ cup soft brown sugar

A little clear honey for glazing

Mix together 50 g/2 oz/¼ cup of the flour, the caster sugar, yeast and a little of the milk and leave in a warm place for 20 minutes until frothy. Mix together the remaining flour and salt and rub in the butter or margarine. Blend in the egg, the yeast mixture and the remaining warm milk and mix to a dough. Knead until elastic and no longer sticky. Place in an oiled bowl, cover with oiled clingfilm (plastic wrap) and leave in a warm place for about 1 hour until doubled in size.

Knead again and roll out to a 33 x 23 cm/13 x 9 in rectangle. Mix together all the filling ingredients except the honey and spread over the dough. Roll up from one long side and seal the edge with a little water. Cut the roll into nine equal-sized pieces and place in a lightly greased baking tin (pan). Cover and leave in a warm place for 30 minutes until doubled in size.

Bake in a preheated oven at 190°C/ 375°F/gas mark 5 for 25 minutes until golden brown. Remove from the oven and brush with honey, then leave to cool.

Coffee Buns

Makes 16

225 g/8 oz/1 cup butter or margarine

450 g/1 lb/4 cups wholemeal (wholewheat) flour

20 ml/4 tsp baking powder

5 ml/1 tsp salt

225 g/8 oz/1 cup soft brown sugar

2 eggs, lightly beaten

100 g/4 oz/2/3 cup currants

5 ml/1 tsp instant coffee powder

15 ml/1 tbsp hot water

75 ml/5 tbsp clear honey

Rub the butter or margarine into the flour, baking powder and salt until the mixture resembles breadcrumbs. Stir in the sugar. Beat in the eggs to make a soft but not sticky dough, then mix in the currants. Dissolve the coffee powder in the hot water and add to the dough. Shape into 16 flattened balls and place, well apart, on a greased baking (cookie) sheet. Press a finger into the centre of each bun and add a teaspoonful of honey. Bake in a preheated oven at 220°C/425°F/gas mark 7 for 10 minutes until light and golden brown.

Crème Fraîche Bread

Makes two 450 g/1 lb loaves

25 g/1 oz fresh yeast or 40 ml/ 2½ tbsp dried yeast

75 g/3 oz/1/3 cup soft brown sugar

60 ml/4 tbsp warm water

60 ml/4 tbsp crème fraîche, at room temperature

350 g/12 oz/3 cups plain (all-purpose) flour

5 ml/1 tsp salt

A pinch of grated nutmeg

3 eggs

50 g/2 oz/¼ cup butter or margarine

A little milk and sugar for glazing

Blend the yeast with 5 ml/1 tsp of the sugar and the warm water and leave in a warm place for 20 minutes until frothy. Stir the crème fraîche into the yeast. Place the flour, salt and nutmeg in a bowl and make a well in the centre. Mix in the yeast mixture, eggs and butter and work to a soft dough. Knead until smooth and elastic. Place in an oiled bowl, cover with oiled clingfilm (plastic wrap) and leave in a warm place for about 1 hour until doubled in size.

Knead the dough again, then shape into two 450 g/1 lb loaf tins (pans). Cover and leave in a warm place for 35 minutes until doubled in size.

Brush the top of the loaves with a little milk, then sprinkle with sugar. Bake in a preheated oven at 180°C/350°F/gas mark 4 for 30 minutes. Leave to cool in the tin for 10 minutes, then turn out on to a wire rack to finish cooling.

Croissants

Makes 12

25 g/1 oz/2 tbsp lard (shortening)

450 g/1 lb/4 cups strong plain (bread) flour

2.5 ml/½ tsp caster (superfine) sugar

10 ml/2 tsp salt

25 g/1 oz fresh yeast or 40 ml/ 2½ tbsp dried yeast

250 ml/8 fl oz/1 cup warm water

2 eggs, lightly beaten

100 g/4 oz/½ cup butter or margarine, diced

Rub the lard into the flour, sugar and salt until the mixture resembles breadcrumbs, then make a well in the centre. Mix the yeast with the water, and add to the flour with one of the eggs. Work the mixture together until you have a soft dough that leaves the sides of the bowl cleanly. Turn out on to a lightly floured surface and knead until smooth and no longer sticky. Roll out the dough to a 20 x 50 cm/8 x 20 in strip. Dot the top two-thirds of the dough with one-third of the butter or margarine, leaving a thin gap round the edge. Fold the unbuttered part of the dough up over the next one-third, then fold the top one-third down over that. Press the edges together to seal, and give the dough a quarter turn so the folded edge is on your left. Repeat the process with the next one-third of the butter or margarine, fold and repeat once more so that you have used all the fat. Put the folded dough in an oiled polythene bag and chill for 30 minutes.

Roll, fold and turn the dough again three more times without adding any more fat. Return to the bag and chill for 30 minutes.

Roll out the dough to a 40 x 38 cm/ 16 x 15 in rectangle, trim the edges and cut into 12 15 cm/6 in triangles. Brush the triangles with a little beaten egg and roll up from the base, then curve into crescent shapes and place, well apart, on a greased baking (cookie) sheet. Brush the tops with egg, cover and leave in a warm place for about 30 minutes.

Brush the tops with egg again, then bake in a preheated oven at 230°C/425°F/ gas mark 7 for 15–20 minutes until golden and puffy.

Wholemeal Sultana Croissants

Makes 12

25 g/1 oz/2 tbsp lard (shortening)

225 g/8 oz/2 cups strong plain (bread) flour

225 g/8 oz/2 cups wholemeal (wholewheat) flour

10 ml/2 tsp salt

25 g/1 oz fresh yeast or 40 ml/ 2½ tbsp dried yeast

300 ml/½ pt/1¼ cups warm water

2 eggs, lightly beaten

100 g/4 oz/½ cup butter or margarine, diced

45 ml/3 tbsp sultanas (golden raisins)

2.5 ml/½ tsp caster (superfine) sugar

Rub the lard into the flour and salt until the mixture resembles breadcrumbs, then make a well in the centre. Mix the yeast with the water, and add to the flour with one of the eggs. Work the mixture together until you have a soft dough that leaves the sides of the bowl cleanly. Turn out on to a lightly floured surface and knead until smooth and no longer sticky. Roll out the dough to a 20 x 50 cm/8 x 20 in strip. Dot the top two-thirds of the dough with one-third of the butter or margarine, leaving a thin gap round the edge. Fold the unbuttered part of the dough up over the next one-third, then fold the top one-third down over that. Press the edges together to seal, and give the dough a quarter turn so the folded edge is on your left. Repeat the process with the next one-third of the butter or margarine, fold and repeat once more so that you have used all the fat. Put the folded dough in an oiled polythene bag and chill for 30 minutes.

Roll, fold and turn the dough again three more times without adding any more fat. Return to the bag and chill for 30 minutes.

Roll out the dough to a 40 x 38 cm/ 16 x 15 in rectangle, trim the edges and cut into twelve 15 cm/6 in triangles. Brush the triangles with a little beaten egg, sprinkle with sultanas and sugar and roll up from the base, then curve into crescent shapes and place well apart on a greased baking (cookie) sheet. Brush the tops with egg, cover and leave in a warm place for 30 minutes.

Brush the tops with egg again, then bake in a preheated oven at 230°C/425°F/ gas mark 7 for 15–20 minutes until golden and puffy.

Forest Rounds

Makes three 350 g/12 oz loaves

450 g/1 lb/4 cups wholemeal (wholewheat) flour

20 ml/4 tsp baking powder

45 ml/3 tbsp carob powder

5 ml/1 tsp salt

50 g/2 oz/½ cup ground hazelnuts

50 g/2 oz/½ cup chopped mixed nuts

75 g/3 oz/1/3 cup vegetable fat (shortening)

75 g/3 oz/¼ cup clear honey

300 ml/½ pt/1¼ cups milk

2.5 ml/½ tsp vanilla essence (extract)

1 egg, beaten

Mix together the dry ingredients, then rub in the vegetable fat. Dissolve the honey in the milk and vanilla essence and mix into the dry ingredients until you have a soft dough. Shape into three rounds and press to flatten slightly. Cut each loaf partly through into six portions and brush with beaten egg. Place on a greased baking (cookie) sheet and bake in a preheated oven at 230°C/450°F/gas mark 8 for 20 minutes until well risen and golden brown.

Nutty Twist

Makes one 450 g/1 lb loaf

For the dough:

15 g/½ oz fresh yeast or 20 ml/ 4 tsp dried yeast

40 g/1½ oz/3 tbsp caster (superfine) sugar

100 ml/3½ fl oz/6 ½ tbsp warm milk

350 g/12 oz/3 cups strong plain (bread) flour

2.5 ml/½ tsp salt

50 g/2 oz/¼ cup butter or margarine, melted

1 egg

For the filling and glaze:

100 g/4 oz/1 cup ground almonds

2 egg whites

50 g/2 oz/¼ cup caster (superfine) sugar

2.5 ml/½ tsp ground cinnamon

100 g/4 oz/1 cup ground hazelnuts

1 egg yolk

To make the dough, blend the yeast with 5 ml/1 tsp of the sugar and a little of the milk and leave in a warm place for 20 minutes until frothy. Mix the flour and salt in a bowl and make a well in the centre. Mix in the yeast mixture, the remaining sugar and milk, the melted butter or margarine and the egg and mix to a smooth dough. Knead until elastic and no longer sticky. Place in an oiled bowl, cover with oiled clingfilm (plastic wrap) and leave in a warm place for about 1 hour until doubled in size.

Roll out the dough on a lightly floured surface to a 30 x 40 cm/12 x 16 in rectangle. Mix together the filling ingredients, except the egg yolk, until you have a smooth paste, then spread over the dough, just short of the edges. Brush the edges with a little of the egg yolk, then roll up the dough from the long side. Cut the dough exactly in half lengthways, then twist the two pieces together, sealing the ends. Place on a greased baking (cookie) sheet, cover and leave in a warm place for 30 minutes until doubled in size. Brush with egg yolk and bake in a preheated oven at 190°C/375°F/gas mark 5 for 30 minutes until golden brown.

Orange Buns

Makes 24

For the dough:
25 g/1 oz fresh yeast or 40 ml/ 2½ tbsp dried yeast

120 ml/4 fl oz/½ cup warm water

75 g/3 oz/1/3 cup caster (superfine) sugar

100 g/4 oz/½ cup lard (shortening), diced

5 ml/1 tsp salt

250 ml/8 fl oz/1 cup warm milk

60 ml/4 tbsp orange juice

30 ml/2 tbsp grated orange rind

2 eggs, beaten

675 g/1½ lb/6 cups strong plain (bread) flour

For the icing (frosting):
250 g/9 oz/1½ cups icing (confectioners') sugar

5 ml/1 tsp grated orange rind

30 ml/2 tbsp orange juice

To make the dough, dissolve the yeast in the warm water with 5 ml/1 tsp of the sugar and leave until frothy. Mix the lard into the remaining sugar and the salt. Stir in the milk, orange juice, rind and eggs, then blend in the yeast mixture. Gradually add the flour and mix to a firm dough. Knead well. Place in a greased bowl, cover with oiled clingfilm (plastic wrap) and leave in a warm place for about 1 hour until doubled in size.

Roll out to about 2 cm/¾ in thick and cut into rounds with a biscuit (cookie) cutter. Place a little way apart on a greased baking (cookie) sheet and leave in a warm place 25 minutes. Leave to cool.

To make the icing, place the sugar in a bowl and mix in the orange rind. Gradually mix in the orange juice until you have a firm icing. Spoon over the buns when cool and leave to set.

Pain Chocolat

Makes 12

25 g/1 oz/2 tbsp lard (shortening)

450 g/1 lb/4 cups strong plain (bread) flour

2.5 ml/½ tsp caster (superfine) sugar

10 ml/2 tsp salt

25 g/1 oz fresh yeast or 40 ml/ 2½ tbsp dried yeast

250 ml/8 fl oz/1 cup warm water

2 eggs, lightly beaten

100 g/4 oz/½ cup butter or margarine, diced

100 g/4 oz/1 cup plain (semi-sweet) chocolate, broken into 12 pieces

Rub the lard into the flour, sugar and salt until the mixture resembles breadcrumbs, then make a well in the centre. Mix the yeast with the water, and add to the flour with one of the eggs. Work the mixture together until you have a soft dough which leaves the sides of the bowl cleanly. Turn out on to a lightly floured surface and knead until smooth and no longer sticky. Roll out the dough to a 20 x 50 cm/8 x 20 in strip. Dot the top two-thirds of the dough with one-third of the butter or margarine, leaving a thin gap round the edge. Fold the unbuttered part of the dough up over the next one-third, then fold the top one-third down over that, Press the edges together to seal, and give the dough a quarter turn so the folded edge is on your left. Repeat the process with the next one-third of the butter or margarine, fold and repeat once more so that you have used all the fat. Put the folded dough in an oiled polythene bag and chill for 30 minutes.

Roll, fold and turn the dough again three more times without adding any more fat. Return to the bag and chill for 30 minutes.

Divide the dough into 12 pieces and roll out into rectangles about 5 cm/2 in wide and 5 mm/¼ in thick. Place a piece of chocolate in the centre of each and roll up, enclosing the chocolate. Place well apart on a greased baking (cookie) sheet. Brush the tops with egg, cover and leave in a warm place for 30 minutes.

Brush the tops with egg again, then bake in a preheated oven at 230°C/425°F/ gas mark 7 for 15–20 minutes until golden and puffy.

Pandolce

Makes two 675 g/1½ lb loaves

175 g/6 oz/1 cup raisins

45 ml/3 tbsp Marsala or sweet sherry

25 g/1 oz fresh yeast or 40 ml/2½ tbsp dried yeast

175 g/6 oz/¾ cup caster (superfine) sugar

400 ml/14 fl oz/1¾ cups warm milk

900 g/2 lb/8 cups plain (all-purpose) flour

A pinch of salt

45 ml/3 tbsp orange flower water

75 g/3 oz/1/3 cup butter or margarine, melted

50 g/2 oz/½ cup pine nuts

50 g/2 oz/½ cup pistachio nuts

10 ml/2 tsp crushed fennel seeds

50 g/2 oz/1/3 cup crystallised (candied) lemon rind, chopped

Grated rind of 1 orange

Mix the raisins and Marsala and leave to soak. Blend the yeast with 5 ml/ 1 tsp of the sugar and a little of the warm milk and leave in a warm place for 20 minutes until frothy. Mix the flour, salt and remaining sugar in a bowl and make a well in the centre. Mix in the yeast mixture, the remaining warm milk and the orange flower water. Add the melted butter or margarine and mix to a soft dough. Knead on a lightly floured surface until elastic and no longer sticky. Place in an oiled bowl, cover with oiled clingfilm (plastic wrap) and leave in a warm place for about 1 hour until doubled in size.

Press or roll out the dough on a lightly floured surface to about 1 cm/½ in thick. Sprinkle with the raisins, nuts, fennel seeds, lemon and orange rinds. Roll up the dough, then press or roll out and roll up again. Shape into a round and place on a greased baking (cookie) sheet. Cover with oiled clingfilm and leave in a warm place for about 1 hour until doubled in size.

Make a triangular cut on the top of the loaf, then bake in a preheated oven at 190°C/375°F/gas mark 5 for 20 minutes. Reduce the oven temperature to 160°C/ 325°F/gas mark 3 and bake for a further 1 hour until golden and hollow-sounding when tapped on the base.

Panettone

Makes one 23 cm/9 in cake

40 g/1½ oz fresh yeast or 60 ml/ 4 tbsp dried yeast

150 g/5 oz/2/3 cup caster (superfine) sugar

300 ml/½ pt/1¼ cups warm milk

225 g/8 oz/1 cup butter or margarine, melted

5 ml/1 tsp salt

Grated rind of 1 lemon

A pinch of grated nutmeg

6 egg yolks

675 g/1½ lb/6 cups strong plain (bread) flour

175 g/6 oz/1 cup raisins

175 g/6 oz/1 cup chopped mixed (candied) peel

75 g/3 oz/¼ cup almonds, chopped

Blend the yeast with 5 ml/1 tsp of the sugar with a little of the warm milk and leave in a warm place for 20 minutes until frothy. Mix the melted butter with the remaining sugar, the salt, lemon rind, nutmeg and egg yolks. Stir the mixture into the flour with the yeast mixture and blend to a smooth dough. Knead until no longer sticky. Place in an oiled bowl, cover with oiled clingfilm (plastic wrap) and leave in a warm place for 20 minutes. Mix together the raisins, mixed peel and almonds and work into the dough. Cover again and leave in a warm place for a further 30 minutes.

Knead the dough lightly, then shape into a greased and lined 23 cm/9 in deep cake tin (pan). Cover and leave in a warm place for 30 minutes until the dough rises well above the top of the tin. Bake in a preheated oven at 190°C/375°F/gas mark 5 for 1½ hours until a skewer inserted in the centre comes out clean.

Apple and Date Loaf

Makes one 900 g/2 lb loaf

350 g/12 oz/3 cups self-raising (self-rising) flour

50 g/2 oz/¼ cup soft brown sugar

5 ml/1 tsp mixed (apple-pie) spice

5 ml/1 tsp ground cinnamon

2.5 ml/½ tsp grated nutmeg

A pinch of salt

1 large cooking (tart) apple, peeled, cored and chopped

175 g/6 oz/1 cup stoned (pitted) dates, chopped

Grated rind of ½ lemon

2 eggs, lightly beaten

150 ml/¼ pt/2/3 cup plain yoghurt

Mix together the dry ingredients, then stir in the apple, dates and lemon rind. Make a well in the centre, add the eggs and yoghurt and gradually mix to a dough. Turn out on to a lightly floured surface and shape into a greased and floured 900 g/2 lb loaf tin (pan). Bake in a preheated oven at 160°C/325°F/gas mark 3 for 1½ hours until well risen and golden brown. Leave to cool in the tin for 5 minutes, then turn out on to a wire rack to finish cooling.

Apple and Sultana Bread

Makes three 350 g/12 oz loaves

25 g/1 oz fresh yeast or 40 ml/2½ tbsp dried yeast

10 ml/2 tsp malt extract

375 ml/13 fl oz/1½ cups warm water

450 g/1 lb/4 cups wholemeal (wholewheat) flour

5 ml/1 tsp soya flour

50 g/2 oz/½ cup rolled oats

2.5 ml/½ tsp salt

25 g/1 oz/2 tbsp soft brown sugar

15 ml/1 tbsp lard (shortening)

225 g/8 oz cooking (tart) apples, peeled, cored and chopped

400 g/14 oz/21/3 cups sultanas (golden raisins)

2.5 ml/½ tsp ground cinnamon

1 egg, beaten

Blend the yeast with the malt extract and a little of the warm water and leave in a warm place until frothy. Mix together the flour, oats, salt and sugar, rub in the lard and make a well in the centre. Mix in the yeast mixture and the remaining warm water and knead to a smooth dough. Mix in the apples, sultanas and cinnamon. Knead until elastic and no longer sticky. Place the dough in an oiled bowl and cover with oiled clingfilm (plastic wrap). Leave in a warm place for 1 hour until doubled in size.

Knead the dough lightly, then shape into three rounds and flatten slightly, then place on a greased baking (cookie) sheet. Brush the tops with beaten egg and bake in a preheated oven at 230°C/450°F/gas mark 8 for 35 minutes until well risen and hollow-sounding when tapped on the base.

Apple and Cinnamon Surprises

Makes 10

For the dough:

25 g/1 oz fresh yeast or 40 ml/2½ tbsp dried yeast

75 g/3 oz/1/3 cup soft brown sugar

300 ml/½ pt/1¼ cups warm water

450 g/1 lb/4 cups wholemeal (wholewheat) flour

2.5 ml/½ tsp salt

25 g/1 oz/¼ cup milk powder (non-fat dry milk)

5 ml/1 tsp ground mixed (apple-pie) spice

5 ml/1 tsp ground cinnamon

75 g/3 oz/1/3 cup butter or margarine

15 ml/1 tbsp grated orange rind

1 egg

For the filling:

450 g/1 lb cooking (tart) apples, peeled, cored and coarsely chopped

75 g/3 oz/½ cup sultanas (golden raisins)

5 ml/1 tsp ground cinnamon

For the glaze:

15 ml/1 tbsp clear honey

30 ml/2 tbsp caster (superfine) sugar

To make the dough, blend the yeast with a little of the sugar and a little of the warm water and leave in a warm place for 20 minutes until frothy. Mix together the flour, salt, milk powder and spices. Rub in the butter or margarine, then stir in the orange rind and make a well in the centre. Add the yeast mixture, the remaining

51

warm water and the egg and mix to a smooth dough. Place in an oiled bowl, cover with oiled clingfilm (plastic wrap) and leave in a warm place for 1 hour until doubled in size.

To make the filling, cook the apples and sultanas in a pan with the cinnamon and a little water until soft and puréed.

Shape the dough into 10 rolls, press your finger into the centre and spoon in some of the filling, then close the dough around the filling. Arrange on a greased baking (cookie) sheet, Cover with oiled clingfilm and leave in a warm place for 40 minutes. Bake in a preheated oven at 230°C/450°F/gas mark 8 for 15 minutes until well risen. Brush with the honey, sprinkle with the sugar and leave to cool.

Apricot Tea Bread

Makes one 900 g/2 lb loaf

225 g/8 oz/2 cups self-raising (self-rising) flour

100 g/4 oz/2/3 cup dried apricots

50 g/2 oz/½ cup almonds, chopped

50 g/2 oz/¼ cup soft brown sugar

50 g/2 oz/¼ cup butter or margarine

100 g/4 oz/1/3 cup golden (light corn) syrup

1 egg

75 ml/5 tbsp milk

Soak the apricots in hot water for 1 hour, then drain and chop.

Mix together the flour, apricots, almonds and sugar. Melt the butter or margarine and syrup. Add to the dry ingredients with the egg and milk. Spoon into a greased and lined 900 g/2 lb loaf tin (pan) and bake in a preheated oven at 180°C/350°F/gas mark 4 for 1 hour until golden brown and firm to the touch.

Apricot and Orange Loaf

Makes one 900 g/2 lb loaf

175 g/6 oz/1 cup no-need-to-soak dried apricots, chopped

150 ml/¼ pt/2/3 cup orange juice

400 g/14 oz/3½ cups plain (all-purpose) flour

175 g/6 oz/¾ cup caster (superfine) sugar

100 g/4 oz/2/3 cup raisins

7.5 ml/1½ tsp baking powder

2.5 ml/½ tsp bicarbonate of soda (baking soda)

2.5 ml/½ tsp salt

Grated rind of 1 orange

1 egg, lightly beaten

25 g/1 oz/2 tbsp butter or margarine, melted

Soak the apricots in the orange juice. Place the dry ingredients and orange rind in a bowl and make a well in the centre. Mix in the apricots and orange juice, egg and melted butter or margarine and work to a stiff mixture. Spoon into a greased and lined 900 g/2 lb loaf tin (pan) and bake in a preheated oven at 180°C/350°F/gas mark 4 for 1 hour until golden and firm to the touch.

Apricot and Walnut Loaf

Makes one 900 g/2 lb loaf

15 g/½ oz fresh yeast or 20 ml/4 tsp dried yeast

30 ml/2 tbsp clear honey

300 ml/½ pt/1¼ cups warm water

25 g/1 oz/2 tbsp butter or margarine

225 g/8 oz/2 cups wholemeal (wholewheat) flour

225 g/8 oz/2 cups plain (all-purpose) flour

5 ml/1 tsp salt

75 g/3 oz/¾ cup walnuts, chopped

175 g/6 oz/1 cup ready-to-eat dried apricots, chopped

Blend the yeast with a little of the honey and a little of the water and leave in a warm place for 20 minutes until frothy. Rub the butter or margarine into the flours and salt and make a well in the centre. Mix in the yeast mixture and the remaining honey and water and mix to a dough. Mix in the walnuts and apricots and knead until smooth and no longer sticky. Place in an oiled bowl, cover and leave in a warm place for 1 hour until doubled in size.

Knead the dough again and shape into a greased 900 g/2 lb loaf tin (pan). Cover with oiled clingfilm (plastic wrap) and leave in a warm place for about 20 minutes until the dough has risen just above the top of the tin. Bake in a preheated oven at 220°C/425°F/gas mark 7 for 30 minutes until golden brown and hollow-sounding when tapped on the base.

Autumn Crown

Makes one large ring loaf

For the dough:

450 g/1 lb/4 cups wholemeal (wholewheat) flour

20 ml/4 tsp baking powder

75 g/3 oz/1/3 cup soft brown sugar

5 ml/1 tsp salt

2.5 ml/½ tsp ground mace

75 g/3 oz/1/3 cup vegetable fat (shortening)

3 egg whites

300 ml/½ pt/1¼ cups milk

For the filling:

175 g/6 oz/1½ cups wholemeal (wholewheat) cake crumbs

50 g/2 oz/½ cup ground hazelnuts or almonds

50 g/2 oz/¼ cup soft brown sugar

75 g/3 oz/½ cup crystallised (candied) ginger, chopped

30 ml/2 tbsp rum or brandy

1 egg, lightly beaten

To glaze:

15 ml/1 tbsp honey

To make the dough, mix together the dry ingredients and rub in the fat. Blend together the egg whites and milk and combine with the mixture until you have a soft, pliable dough.

Mix together the filling ingredients, using just enough of the egg to make a spreading consistency. Roll out the dough on a lightly floured surface to a 20 x 30 cm/8 x 10 in rectangle. Spread the filling over all but the top 2.5 cm/1 in along the long edge. Roll up from the opposite edge, like a Swiss (jelly) roll, and moisten the plain strip of dough to seal. Moisten each end and shape the roll into a circle, sealing the ends together. With sharp scissors, make little cuts around the top for decoration. Place on a greased baking (cookie) sheet and brush with the remaining egg. Leave to rest for 15 minutes.

Bake in a preheated oven at 230°C/450°F/gas mark 8 for 25 minutes until golden brown. Brush with honey and leave to cool.

Banana Loaf

Makes one 900 g/2 lb loaf

75 g/3 oz/1/3 cup butter or margarine, softened

175 g/6 oz/2/3 cup caster (superfine) sugar

2 eggs, lightly beaten

450 g/1 lb ripe bananas, mashed

200 g/7 oz/1¾ cup self-raising (self-rising) flour

75 g/3 oz/¾ cup walnuts, chopped

100 g/4 oz/2/3 cup sultanas (golden raisins)

50 g/2 oz/½ cup glacé (candied) cherries

2.5 ml/½ tsp bicarbonate of soda (baking soda)

A pinch of salt

Cream together the butter or margarine and sugar until pale and fluffy. Gradually beat in the eggs, then stir in the bananas. Mix in the remaining ingredients until well blended. Spoon into a greased and lined 900 g/2 lb loaf tin (pan) and bake in a preheated oven at 180°C/350°C/gas mark 4 for 1¼ hours until well risen and firm to the touch.

Wholemeal Banana Bread

Makes one 900 g/2 lb loaf

100 g/4 oz/½ cup butter or margarine, softened

50 g/2 oz/¼ cup soft brown sugar

2 eggs, lightly beaten

3 bananas, mashed

175 g/6 oz/1½ cups wholemeal (wholewheat) flour

100 g/4 oz/1 cup oat flour

5 ml/1 tsp baking powder

5 ml/1 tsp ground mixed (apple-pie) spice

30 ml/2 tbsp milk

Cream together the butter or margarine and sugar until light and fluffy. Gradually beat in the eggs, stir in the bananas, then fold in the flours, baking powder and mixed spice. Add enough of the milk to make a soft mixture. Spoon into a greased and lined 900 g/2 lb loaf tin (pan) and level the surface. Bake in a preheated oven at 190°C/375°F/gas mark 5 until risen and golden brown.

Banana and Nut Bread

Makes one 900 g/2 lb loaf

50 g/2 oz/¼ cup butter or margarine

225 g/8 oz/2 cups self-raising (self-rising) flour

50 g/2 oz/¼ cup caster (superfine) sugar

50 g/2 oz/½ cup chopped mixed nuts

1 egg, lightly beaten

75 g/3 oz/1/3 cup golden (light corn) syrup

2 bananas, mashed

15 ml/1 tbsp milk

Rub the butter or margarine into the flour, then stir in the sugar and nuts. Mix in the egg, syrup and bananas and enough of the milk to give a soft mixture. Spoon into a greased and lined 900 g/2 lb loaf tin (pan) and bake in a preheated oven at 180°C/350°F/gas mark 4 for about 1 hour until firm and golden brown. Store for 24 hours before serving sliced and buttered.

Bara Brith

Makes three 450 g/1 lb loaves

450 g/1 lb/2¾ cups dried mixed fruit (fruit cake mix)

250 ml/8 fl oz/1 cup strong cold tea

30 ml/2 tbsp dried yeast

175 g/6 oz/¾ cup soft brown sugar

250 g/12 oz/3 cups wholemeal (wholewheat) flour

350 g/12 oz/3 cups strong plain (bread) flour

10 ml/2 tsp ground mixed (apple-pie) spice

100 g/4 oz/½ cup butter or margarine, melted

2 eggs, beaten

2.5 ml/½ tsp salt

15 ml/1 tbsp clear honey

Soak the fruit in the tea for 2 hours. Warm 30 ml/2 tbsp of the tea and mix with the yeast and 5 ml/1 tsp of the sugar. Leave in a warm place until frothy. Mix together the dry ingredients, then blend in the yeast mixture and all remaining ingredients except the honey and mix to a dough. Turn out on to a lightly floured surface and knead gently until smooth and elastic. Divide between three greased and lined 450 g/1 lb loaf tins (pans). Cover with oiled clingfilm (plastic wrap) and leave in a warm place for 1 hour until the dough has risen above the top of the tins.

Bake in a preheated oven at 200°C/400°F/gas mark 6 for 15 minutes, then reduce the oven temperature to 180°C/350°F/gas mark 4 for a further 45 minutes until golden and hollow-sounding when tapped on the base. Warm the honey and brush over the tops of the warm loaves.

Bath Buns

Makes 12 buns

500 g/1 lb/4 cups strong plain (bread) flour

25 g/1 oz fresh yeast or 40 ml/2½ tbsp dried yeast

150 ml/¼ pt/2/3 cup warm milk

75 g/3 oz/1/3 cup caster (superfine) sugar

150 ml/¼ pt/2/3 cup warm water

5 ml/1 tsp salt

50 g/2 oz/¼ cup butter or margarine

2 eggs, beaten

175 g/6 oz/1 cup sultanas (golden raisins)

50 g/2 oz/1/3 cup chopped mixed peel

Beaten egg for glazing

Preserving sugar, crushed, for sprinkling

Place a quarter of the flour in a bowl and make a well in the centre. Mix the yeast with half the milk and 5 ml/1 tsp of the sugar and pour into the well. Add the remaining liquid. Stir together and leave in a warm place for 35 minutes until frothy. Place the remaining flour in a bowl with the salt. Stir in the remaining sugar, then rub in the butter or margarine until the mixture resembles breadcrumbs. Pour in the yeast mixture and eggs and beat well. Stir in the sultanas and mixed peel. Cover with oiled clingfilm (plastic wrap) and leave in a warm place until doubled in size.

Knead the dough well and divide into 12 pieces. Shape into a round and place on a greased baking (cookie) sheet. Cover with oiled clingfilm and leave in a warm place for 15 minutes. Brush with beaten egg and sprinkle with crushed sugar. Bake in a preheated oven at 200°C/400°F/gas mark 6 for 15–20 minutes until golden.

Cherry and Honey Loaf

Makes one 900 g/2 lb loaf

175 g/6 oz/¾ cup butter or margarine, softened

75 g/3 oz/1/3 cup soft brown sugar

60 ml/4 tbsp clear honey

2 eggs, beaten

100 g/4 oz/2 cups wholemeal (wholewheat) flour

10 ml/2 tsp baking powder

100 g/4 oz/½ cup glacé (candied) cherries, chopped

45 ml/3 tbsp milk

Cream together the butter or margarine, sugar and honey until light and fluffy. Gradually stir in the eggs, beating well after each addition. Mix in the remaining ingredients to make a soft mixture. Spoon into a greased and lined 900 g/2 lb loaf tin (pan) and bake in a preheated oven at 180°C/350°F/gas mark 4 for 1 hour until a skewer inserted in the centre comes out clean. Serve sliced and buttered.

Cinnamon and Nutmeg Rolls

Makes 24

15 ml/1 tbsp dried yeast

120 ml/4 fl oz/½ cup milk, boiled

50 g/2 oz/¼ cup caster (superfine) sugar

50 g/2 oz/¼ cup lard (shortening)

5 ml/1 tsp salt

120 ml/4 fl oz/½ cup warm water

2.5 ml/½ tsp grated nutmeg

1 egg, beaten

400 g/14 oz/3½ cups strong plain (bread) flour

45 ml/3 tbsp butter or margarine, melted

175 g/6 oz/¾ cup soft brown sugar

10 ml/2 tsp ground cinnamon

75 g/3 oz/½ cup raisins

Dissolve the yeast in the warm milk with a teaspoon of the caster sugar and leave until frothy. Mix together the remaining caster sugar, the lard and salt. Pour in the water and stir until blended. Stir in the yeast mixture, then gradually add the nutmeg, egg and flour. Knead to a smooth dough. Place in a greased bowl, cover with oiled clingfilm (plastic wrap) and leave in a warm place for about 1 hour until doubled in size.

Divide the dough in half and roll out on a lightly floured surface into rectangles about 5 mm/¼ in thick. Brush with melted butter and sprinkle with the brown sugar, cinnamon and raisins. Roll up from the longer size and cut each roll into 12 slices 1 cm/½ in thick. Place the slices a little way apart on a greased baking (cookie) sheet and leave in a warm place for 1 hour. Bake in a preheated oven at 190°C/375°F/gas mark 5 for 20 minutes until well risen.

Cranberry Bread

Makes one 450 g/1 lb loaf

225 g/8 oz/2 cups plain (all-purpose) flour

2.5 ml/½ tsp salt

2.5 ml/½ tsp bicarbonate of soda (baking soda)

225 g/8 oz/1 cup caster (superfine) sugar

7.5 ml/1½ tsp baking powder

Juice and grated rind of 1 orange

1 egg, beaten

25 g/1 oz/2 tbsp lard (shortening), melted

100 g/4 oz fresh or frozen cranberries, crushed

50 g/2 oz/½ cup walnuts, coarsely chopped

Mix together the dry ingredients in a large bowl. Put the orange juice and rind in a measuring jug and make up to 175 ml/6 fl oz/¾ cup with water. Stir into the dry ingredients with the egg and lard. Stir in the cranberries and nuts. Spoon into a greased 450 g/1 lb loaf tin (pan) and bake in a preheated oven at 160°C/325°F/gas mark 3 for about 1 hour until a skewer inserted in the centre comes out clean. Leave to cool, then keep for 24 hours before cutting.

Date and Butter Loaf

Makes one 900 g/2 lb loaf

For the loaf:

175 g/6 oz/1 cup stoned (pitted) dates, finely chopped

5 ml/1 tsp bicarbonate of soda (baking soda)

250 ml/8 fl oz/1 cup boiling water

75 g/3 oz/1/3 cup butter or margarine, softened

225 g/8 oz/1 cup soft brown sugar

1 egg, lightly beaten

5 ml/1 tsp vanilla essence (extract)

225 g/8 oz/2 cups plain (all-purpose) flour

5 ml/1 tsp baking powder

A pinch of salt

For the topping:

100 g/4 oz/½ cup soft brown sugar

50 g/2 oz/¼ cup butter or margarine

120 ml/4 fl oz/½ cup single (light) cream

To make the loaf, mix together the dates, bicarbonate of soda and boiling water and stir well, then leave to cool. Cream together the butter or margarine and sugar until light and fluffy, then gradually beat in the egg and vanilla essence. Stir in the flour, baking powder and salt. Spoon the mixture into a greased and lined 900 g/2 lb loaf tin (pan) and bake in a preheated oven at 180°C/350°F/gas mark 4 for 1 hour until a skewer inserted in the centre comes out clean.

To make the topping, melt together the sugar, butter or margarine and cream over a low heat until blended, then simmer very gently for 15 minutes, stirring occasionally. Remove the loaf from the tin and pour over the hot topping. Leave to cool.

Date and Banana Bread

Makes one 900 g/2 lb loaf

225 g/8 oz/11/3 cups stoned (pitted) dates, chopped

300 ml/½ pt/1¼ cups milk

5 ml/1 tsp bicarbonate of soda (baking soda)

100 g/4 oz/½ cup butter or margarine

275 g/10 oz/2½ cups self-raising (self-rising) flour

2 ripe bananas, mashed

1 egg, beaten

75 g/3 oz/¾ cup hazelnuts, chopped

30 ml/2 tbsp clear honey

Place the dates, milk and bicarbonate of soda in a pan and bring to the boil, stirring. Leave to cool. Rub the butter or margarine into the flour until the mixture resembles breadcrumbs. Stir in the bananas, egg and most of the hazelnuts, reserving a few for decoration. Spoon into a greased and lined 900 g/2 lb loaf tin (pan) and bake in a preheated oven at 180°C/350°F/gas mark 4 for 1 hour until a skewer inserted in the centre comes out clean. Leave to cool in the tin for 5 minutes, then turn out and remove the lining paper. Warm the honey and brush over the top of the cake. Sprinkle with the reserved nuts and leave to cool completely.

Date and Orange Loaf

Makes one 900 g/2 lb loaf

225 g/8 oz/11/3 cups stoned (pitted) dates, chopped

120 ml/4 fl oz/½ cup water

200 g/7 oz/scant 1 cup soft brown sugar

75 g/3 oz/1/3 cup butter or margarine

Grated rind and juice of 1 orange

1 egg, lightly beaten

225 g/8 oz/2 cups plain (all-purpose) flour

10 ml/2 tsp baking powder

5 ml/1 tsp ground cinnamon

Simmer the dates in the water for 15 minutes until pulpy. Stir in the sugar until dissolved. Remove from the heat and leave to cool slightly. Beat in the butter or margarine, orange rind and juice, then the egg. Beat in the flour, baking powder and cinnamon. Spoon into a greased and lined 900 g/2 lb loaf tin (pan) and bake in a preheated oven at 180°C/350°F/gas mark 4 for 1 hour until a skewer inserted in the centre comes out clean.

Date and Nut Bread

Makes one 900 g/2 lb loaf

250 ml/8 fl oz/1 cup boiling water

225 g/8 oz/11/3 cups stoned (pitted) dates, chopped

10 ml/2 tsp bicarbonate of soda (baking soda)

25 g/1 oz/2 tbsp vegetable fat (shortening)

225 g/8 oz/1 cup soft brown sugar

2 eggs, beaten

225 g/8 oz/2 cups plain (all-purpose) flour

5 ml/1 tsp salt

50 g/2 oz/½ cup pecan nuts, chopped

Pour the boiling water over the dates and bicarbonate of soda and leave until lukewarm. Cream together the vegetable fat and sugar until creamy. Gradually beat in the eggs. Mix the flour with the salt and nuts, then fold into the creamed mixture alternately with the dates and liquid. Spoon into a greased 900 g/2 lb loaf tin (pan) and bake in a preheated oven at 180°C/350°F/gas mark 4 for 1 hour until firm to the touch.

Date Tea Bread

Makes one 900 g/2 lb loaf

225 g/8 oz/2 cups plain (all-purpose) flour

100 g/4 oz/½ cup soft brown sugar

A pinch of salt

5 ml/1 tsp ground mixed (apple-pie) spice

5 ml/1 tsp bicarbonate of soda (baking soda)

50 g/2 oz/¼ cup butter or margarine, melted

15 ml/1 tbsp black treacle (molasses)

150 ml/¼ pt/2/3 cup black tea

1 egg, beaten

75 g/3 oz/½ cup stoned (pitted) dates, chopped

Mix together the flour, sugar, salt, spice and bicarbonate of soda. Stir in the butter, treacle, tea and egg and mix well until smooth. Stir in the dates. Spoon the mixture into a greased and lined 900 g/2 lb loaf tin (pan) and bake in a preheated oven at 180°C/350°F/gas mark 4 for 45 minutes.

Date and Walnut Loaf

Makes one 900 g/2 lb loaf

100 g/4 oz/½ cup butter or margarine

175 g/6 oz/1½ cups wholemeal (wholewheat) flour

50 g/2 oz/½ cup oat flour

10 ml/2 tsp baking powder

5 ml/1 tsp ground mixed (apple-pie) spice

2.5 ml/½ tsp ground cinnamon

50 g/2 oz/¼ cup soft brown sugar

75 g/3 oz/½ cup stoned (pitted) dates, chopped

75 g/3 oz/¾ cup walnuts, chopped

2 eggs, lightly beaten

30 ml/2 tbsp milk

Rub the butter or margarine into the flours, baking powder and spices until the mixture resembles breadcrumbs. Stir in the sugar, dates and walnuts. Mix in the eggs and milk to make a soft dough. Shape the dough into a greased 900 g/2 lb loaf tin (pan) and level the top. Bake in a preheated oven at 160°C/325°F/gas mark 3 for 45 minutes until risen and golden .

Fig Loaf

Makes one 450 g/1 lb loaf

100 g/4 oz/1½ cups bran cereal

100 g/4 oz/½ cup soft brown sugar

100 g/4 oz/2/3 cup dried figs, chopped

30 ml/2 tbsp black treacle (molasses)

250 ml/8 fl oz/1 cup milk

100 g/4 oz/1 cup wholemeal (wholewheat) flour

10 ml/2 tsp baking powder

Mix the cereal, sugar, figs, treacle and milk and leave to stand for 30 minutes. Stir in the flour and baking powder. Spoon into a greased 450 g/1 lb loaf tin (pan) and bake in a preheated oven at 180°C/350°F/gas mark 4 for 45 minutes until firm and a skewer inserted in the centre comes out clean.

Fig and Marsala Bread

Makes one 900 g/2 lb loaf

225 g/8 oz/1 cup unsalted (sweet) butter or margarine, softened

225 g/8 oz/1 cup soft brown sugar

4 eggs, lightly beaten

45 ml/3 tbsp Marsala

5 ml/1 tsp vanilla essence (extract)

200 g/7 oz/1¾ cups plain (all-purpose) flour

A pinch of salt

50 g/2 oz/1/3 cup ready-to-eat dried apricots, chopped

50 g/2 oz/1/3 cup stoned (pitted) dates, chopped

50 g/2 oz/1/3 cup dried figs, chopped

50 g/2 oz/½ cup chopped mixed nuts

Cream together the butter or margarine and sugar until light and fluffy. Gradually add the eggs, then the Marsala and vanilla essence. Mix the flour and salt with the fruit and nuts, then fold into the mixture and mix well. Spoon into a greased and floured 900 g/2 lb loaf tin (pan) and bake in a preheated oven at 180°C/350°F/gas mark 4 for 1 hour. Leave to cool in the tin for 10 minutes, then turn out on to a wire rack to finish cooling.

Honey and Fig Rolls

Makes 12

25 g/1 oz fresh yeast or 40 ml/2½ tbsp dried yeast

75 g/3 oz/¼ cup clear honey

300 ml/½ pt/1¼ cups warm water

100 g/4 oz/2/3 cup dried figs, chopped

15 ml/1 tbsp malt extract

450 g/1 lb/4 cups wholemeal (wholewheat) flour

15 ml/1 tbsp milk powder (non-fat dry milk)

5 ml/1 tsp salt

2.5 ml/½ tsp grated nutmeg

40 g/1½ oz/2½ tbsp butter or margarine

Grated zest of 1 orange

1 egg, beaten

15 ml/1 tbsp sesame seeds

Blend the yeast with 5 ml/1 tsp of the honey and a little of the warm water and leave in a warm place until frothy. Mix the remaining warm water with the figs, malt extract and remaining honey and leave to soak. Mix together the flour, milk powder, salt and nutmeg, then rub in the butter or margarine and stir in the orange rind. Make a well in the centre and pour in the yeast mixture and the fig mixture. Mix to a soft dough and knead until no longer sticky. Place in an oiled bowl, cover with oiled clingfilm (plastic wrap) and leave in a warm place for 1 hour until doubled in size.

Knead lightly, then shape into 12 rolls and arrange on a greased baking (cookie) sheet. Cover with oiled clingfilm and leave in a warm place for 20 minutes. Brush with beaten egg and sprinkle with sesame seeds. Bake in a preheated oven at 230°C/450°F/gas mark 8 for 15 minutes until golden brown and hollow-sounding when tapped on the base.

Hot Cross Buns

Makes 12

For the buns:

450 g/1 lb/4 cups strong (bread) flour

15 ml/1 tbsp dried yeast

A pinch of salt

5 ml/1 tsp ground mixed (apple-pie) spice

50 g/2 oz/¼ cup caster (superfine) sugar

100 g/4 oz/2/3 cup currants

25 g/1 oz/3 tbsp chopped mixed (candied) peel

1 egg, beaten

250 ml/8 fl oz/1 cup milk

50 g/2 oz/¼ cup butter or margarine, melted

For the crosses:

25 g/1 oz/¼ cup plain (all-purpose) flour

15 ml/1 tbsp water

A little beaten egg

For the glaze:

50 g/2 oz/¼ cup caster (superfine) sugar

150 ml/¼ pt/2/3 cup water

To make the buns, mix together the dry ingredients, currants and mixed peel. Stir in the egg, milk and melted butter and mix to a firm dough that comes away from the sides of the bowl. Turn out on to a lightly floured surface and knead for 5 minutes until smooth and elastic. Divide into 12 and roll into balls. Place well apart on a greased baking (cookie) sheet, cover with oiled clingfilm (plastic wrap) and leave in a warm place for about 45 minutes until doubled in size.

Put the flour for the cross in a small bowl and gradually mix in enough of the water to make a dough. Roll out to a long strand. Brush the tops of the buns with beaten egg, then gently press a cross of dough cut from the long strand into each one. Bake in a preheated oven at 220°C/425°F/gas mark 7 for 20 minutes until golden brown.

To make the glaze, dissolve the sugar in the water, then boil until syrupy. Brush over the hot buns, then transfer them to a wire rack to cool.

Lincolnshire Plum Bread

Makes three 450 g/1 lb loaves

15 g/½ oz fresh yeast or 20 ml/4 tsp dried yeast

45 ml/3 tbsp soft brown sugar

200 ml/7 fl oz/scant 1 cup warm milk

100 g/4 oz/½ cup butter or margarine

450 g/1 lb/4 cups plain (all-purpose) flour

10 ml/2 tsp baking powder

A pinch of salt

1 egg, beaten

450 g/1 lb/22/3 cups dried mixed fruit (fruit cake mix)

Blend the yeast with 5 ml/1 tsp of the sugar and a little of the warm milk and leave in a warm place for 20 minutes until frothy. Rub the butter or margarine into the flour, baking powder and salt until the mixture resembles breadcrumbs. Stir in the remaining sugar and make a well in the centre. Mix in the yeast mixture, remaining warm milk and the egg, then work in the fruit to make a fairly stiff dough. Shape into three greased 450 g/1 lb loaf tins (pans) and bake in a preheated oven at 150°C/300°F/gas mark 2 for 2 hours until golden brown.

London Buns

Makes 10

50 g/2 oz fresh yeast or 30 ml/2 tbsp dried yeast

75 g/3 oz/1/3 cup soft brown sugar

300 ml/½ pt/1¼ cups warm water

175 g/6 oz/1 cup currants

25 g/1 oz/3 tbsp chopped stoned (pitted) dates

25 g/1 oz/3 tbsp chopped mixed (candied) peel

25 g/1 oz/2 tbsp chopped glacé (candied) cherries

45 ml/3 tbsp orange juice

450 g/1 lb/4 cups wholemeal (wholewheat) flour

2.5 ml/½ tsp salt

25 g/1 oz/¼ cup milk powder (non-fat dry milk)

15 ml/1 tbsp ground mixed (apple-pie) spice

5 ml/1 tsp ground cinnamon

75 g/3 oz/1/3 cup butter or margarine

15 ml/1 tbsp grated orange rind

1 egg

15 ml/1 tbsp clear honey

30 ml/2 tbsp flaked (slivered) almonds

Blend the yeast with a little of the sugar and a little of the warm water and leave in a warm place for 20 minutes until frothy. Soak the currants, dates, mixed peel and cherries in the orange juice. Mix together the flour, salt, milk powder and spices. Rub in the butter or margarine, then stir in the orange rind and make a well in the centre. Add the yeast mixture, the remaining warm water and the egg and mix to a smooth dough. Place in an oiled bowl, cover with clingfilm (plastic wrap) and leave in a warm place for 1 hour until doubled in size.

Shape the dough into 10 rolls and arrange on a greased baking (cookie) sheet. Cover with oiled clingfilm and leave in a warm place for 45 minutes. Bake in a preheated oven at 230°C/450°F/gas mark 8 for 15 minutes until well risen. Brush with the honey, sprinkle with the almonds and leave to cool.

Irish Country Loaf

Makes one 900 g/2 lb loaf

350 g/12 oz/3 cups wholemeal (wholewheat) flour

100 g/4 oz/1 cup oatmeal

100 g/4 oz/2/3 cup sultanas (golden raisins)

15 ml/1 tbsp baking powder

15 ml/1 tbsp caster (superfine) sugar

5 ml/1 tsp bicarbonate of soda (baking soda)

5 ml/1 tsp salt

10 ml/2 tsp ground mixed (apple-pie) spice

Grated rind of ½ lemon

1 egg, beaten

300 ml/½ pt/1¼ cups buttermilk or plain yoghurt

150 ml/¼ pt/2/3 cup water

Mix together all the dry ingredients and lemon rind and make a well in the centre. Beat together the egg, buttermilk or yoghurt and water. Mix into the dry ingredients and work to a soft dough. Knead on a lightly floured surface, then shape into a greased 900 g/2 lb loaf tin (pan). Bake in a preheated oven at 200°C/400°F/gas mark 6 for 1 hour until well risen and firm to the touch.

Malt Loaf

Makes one 450 g/1 lb loaf

25 g/1 oz/2 tbsp butter or margarine

225 g/8 oz/2 cups self-raising (self-rising) flour

25 g/1 oz/2 tbsp soft brown sugar

30 ml/2 tbsp black treacle (molasses)

20 ml/4 tsp malt extract

150 ml/¼ pt/2/3 cup milk

75 g/3 oz/½ cup sultanas (golden raisins)

15 ml/1 tbsp caster (superfine) sugar

30 ml/2 tbsp water

Rub the butter or margarine into the flour, then stir in the brown sugar. Warm the treacle, malt extract and milk, then blend into the dry ingredients with the sultanas and mix to a dough. Turn into a greased 450 g/1 lb loaf tin (pan) and bake in a preheated oven at 160°C/325°F/gas mark 3 for 1 hour until golden. Bring the sugar and water to the boil and boil until syrupy. Brush over the top of the loaf and leave to cool.

Bran Malt Loaf

Makes one 450 g/1 lb loaf

100 g/4 oz/½ cup soft brown sugar

225 g/8 oz/11/3 cups dried mixed fruit (fruit cake mix)

75 g/3 oz All Bran cereal

250 ml/8 fl oz/1 cup milk

5 ml/1 tsp ground mixed (apple-pie) spice

100 g/4 oz/1 cup self-raising (self-rising) flour

Mix together the sugar, fruit, All Bran, milk and spice and leave to soak for 1 hour. Stir in the flour and mix well. Spoon into a greased and lined 450 g/1 lb loaf tin (pan) and bake in a preheated oven at 180°C/350°F/gas mark 4 for 1½ hours until firm to the touch.

Wholemeal Malt Loaf

Makes one 900 g/2 lb loaf

25 g/1 oz/2 tbsp butter or margarine

30 ml/2 tbsp black treacle (molasses)

45 ml/3 tbsp malt extract

150 ml/¼ pt/2/3 cup milk

175 g/6 oz/1½ cups wholemeal (wholewheat) flour

75 g/3 oz/¾ cup oat flour

10 ml/2 tsp baking powder

100 g/4 oz/2/3 cup raisins

Melt the butter or margarine, treacle, malt extract and milk. Pour into the flours, baking powder and raisins and mix to a soft dough. Spoon into a greased 900 g/2 lb loaf tin (pan) and level the surface. Bake in a preheated oven at 200°C/400°F/gas mark 6 for 45 minutes until a skewer inserted in the centre comes out clean.

Freda's Nut Loaf

Makes three 350 g/12 oz loaves

25 g/1 oz fresh yeast or 40 ml/2½ tbsp dried yeast

10 ml/2 tsp malt extract

375 ml/13 fl oz/1½ cups warm water

450 g/1 lb/4 cups wholemeal (wholewheat) flour

5 ml/1 tsp soya flour

50 g/2 oz/½ cup rolled oats

2.5 ml/½ tsp salt

25 g/1 oz/2 tbsp soft brown sugar

15 ml/1 tbsp lard (shortening)

100 g/4 oz/1 cup chopped mixed nuts

175 g/6 oz/1 cup currants

50 g/2 oz/1/3 cup stoned (pitted) dates, chopped

50 g/2 oz/1/3 cup raisins

2.5 ml/½ tsp ground cinnamon

1 egg, beaten

45 ml/3 tbsp flaked (slivered) almonds

Blend the yeast with the malt extract and a little of the warm water and leave in a warm place until frothy. Mix together the flours, oats, salt and sugar, rub in the lard and make a well in the centre. Mix in the yeast mixture and the remaining warm water and knead to a smooth dough. Mix in the nuts, currants, dates, raisins and cinnamon. Knead until elastic and no longer sticky. Place the dough in an oiled bowl and cover with oiled clingfilm (plastic wrap). Leave in a warm place for 1 hour until doubled in size.

Knead the dough lightly, then shape into three rounds and flatten slightly, then place on a greased baking (cookie) sheet. Brush the tops with beaten egg and sprinkle with the almonds. Bake in a preheated oven at 230°C/450°F/gas mark 8 for 35 minutes until well risen and hollow-sounding when tapped on the base.

Brazil Nut and Date Loaf

Makes three 350 g/12 oz loaves

25 g/1 oz fresh yeast or 40 ml/2½ tbsp dried yeast

10 ml/2 tsp malt extract

375 ml/13 fl oz/1½ cups warm water

450 g/1 lb/4 cups wholemeal (wholewheat) flour

5 ml/1 tsp soya flour

50 g/2 oz/½ cup rolled oats

2.5 ml/½ tsp salt

25 g/1 oz/2 tbsp soft brown sugar

15 ml/1 tbsp lard (shortening)

100 g/4 oz/1 cup brazil nuts, chopped

250 g/9 oz/1½ cup stoned (pitted) dates, chopped

2.5 ml/½ tsp ground cinnamon

1 egg, beaten

45 ml/3 tbsp sliced brazil nuts

Blend the yeast with the malt extract and a little of the warm water and leave in a warm place until frothy. Mix together the flours, oats, salt and sugar, rub in the lard and make a well in the centre. Mix in the yeast mixture and the remaining warm water and knead to a smooth dough. Mix in the nuts, dates and cinnamon. Knead until elastic and no longer sticky. Place the dough in an oiled bowl and cover with oiled clingfilm (plastic wrap). Leave in a warm place for 1 hour until doubled in size.

Knead the dough lightly, shape into three rounds and flatten slightly, then place on a greased baking (cookie) sheet. Brush the tops with beaten egg and sprinkle with the sliced brazil nuts. Bake in a preheated oven at 230°C/450°F/gas mark 8 for 35 minutes until well risen and hollow-sounding when tapped on the base.

Panastan Fruit Bread

Makes three 175 g/12 oz loaves

25 g/1 oz fresh yeast or 40 ml/2½ tbsp dried yeast

150 ml/¼ pt/2/3 cup warm water

60 ml/4 tbsp clear honey

5 ml/1 tsp malt extract

15 ml/1 tbsp sunflower seeds

15 ml/1 tbsp sesame seeds

25 g/1 oz/¼ cup wheatgerm

450 g/1 lb/4 cups wholemeal (wholewheat) flour

5 ml/1 tsp salt

50 g/2 oz/¼ cup butter or margarine

175 g/6 oz/1 cup sultanas (golden raisins)

25 g/1 oz/3 tbsp chopped mixed (candied) peel

1 egg, beaten

Blend the yeast with a little of the warm water and 5 ml/1 tsp of the honey and leave in a warm place for 20 minutes until frothy. Mix the remaining honey and the malt extract into the remaining warm water. Toast the sunflower and sesame seeds and the wheatgerm in a dry pan, shaking until golden brown. Place in a bowl with the flour and salt and rub in the butter or margarine. Stir in the sultanas and mixed peel and make a well in the centre. Add the yeast mixture, the water mixture and the egg and knead to a smooth dough. Place in an oiled bowl, cover with oiled clingfilm (plastic wrap) and leave in a warm place for 1 hour until doubled in size.

Knead lightly, then shape into three loaves and place on a greased baking (cookie) sheet or in greased baking tins (pans). Cover with oiled clingfilm and leave in a warm place for 20 minutes. Bake in a preheated oven at 230°C/450°F/gas mark 8 for 40 minutes until golden brown and hollow-sounding when tapped on the base.

Pumpkin Loaf

Makes two 450 g/1 lb loaves

350 g/12 oz/1½ cups caster (superfine) sugar

120 ml/4 fl oz/½ cup oil

2.5 ml/½ tsp grated nutmeg

5 ml/1 tsp ground cinnamon

5 ml/1 tsp salt

2 eggs, beaten

225 g/8 oz/1 cup cooked, mashed pumpkin

60 ml/4 tbsp water

2.5 ml/½ tsp bicarbonate of soda (baking soda)

1.5 ml/¼ tsp baking powder

175 g/6 oz/1½ cups plain (all-purpose) flour

Mix together the sugar, oil, nutmeg, cinnamon, salt and eggs and beat well. Stir in the remaining ingredients and mix to a smooth batter. Pour into two greased 450 g/1 lb loaf tins (pans) and bake in a preheated oven at 180°C/350°F/gas mark 4 for 1 hour until a skewer inserted in the centre comes out clean.

Raisin Bread

Makes two 450 g/1 lb loaves

15 ml/1 tbsp dried yeast

120 ml/4 fl oz/½ cup warm water

250 ml/8 fl oz/1 cup warm milk

60 ml/4 tbsp oil

50 g/2 oz/¼ cup sugar

1 egg, beaten

10 ml/2 tsp ground cinnamon

5 ml/1 tsp salt

225 g/8 oz/11/3 cups raisins, soaked in cold water overnight

550 g/1¼ lb/5 cups strong plain (bread) flour

Dissolve the yeast in the warm water and leave until frothy. Mix together the milk, oil, sugar, egg, cinnamon and salt. Drain the raisins and stir them into the mixture. Stir in the yeast mixture. Gradually work in the flour and mix to a stiff dough. Place in a greased bowl and cover with oiled clingfilm (plastic wrap). Leave in a warm place for about 1 hour to rise until doubled in size.

Knead again and shape into two greased 450 g/1 lb loaf tins (pans). Cover with oiled clingfilm and leave in a warm place again until the dough rises above the top of the tins. Bake in a preheated oven at 150°C/300°F/gas mark 2 for 1 hour until golden.

Raisin Soak

Makes two 450 g/l lb loaves

450 g/1 lb/4 cups plain (all-purpose) flour

2.5 ml/½ tsp salt

5 ml/1 tsp ground mixed (apple-pie) spice

225 g/8 oz/11/3 cups raisins, chopped

10 ml/2 tsp bicarbonate of soda (baking soda)

100 g/4 oz/½ cup butter or margarine, melted

225 g/8 oz/1 cup caster (superfine) sugar

450 ml/¾ pt/2 cups milk

15 ml/1 tbsp lemon juice

30 ml/2 tbsp apricot jam (conserve), sieved (strained)

Mix together the flour, salt, mixed spice and raisins. Stir the bicarbonate of soda into the melted butter until blended, then stir all the ingredients together until well mixed. Cover and leave to stand overnight.

Spoon the mixture into two greased and lined 450 g/1 lb loaf tins (pans) and bake in a preheated oven at 180°C/350°F/gas mark 4 for 1 hour until a skewer inserted in the centre comes out clean.

Rhubarb and Date Bread

Makes one 900 g/2 lb loaf

225 g/8 oz rhubarb, chopped

50 g/2 oz/¼ cup butter or margarine

225 g/8 oz/2 cups plain (all-purpose) flour

15 ml/1 tbsp baking powder

175 g/6 oz/1 cup dates, stoned (pitted) and finely chopped

1 egg, beaten

60 ml/4 tbsp milk

Wash the rhubarb and cook gently in just the water clinging to the pieces until you have a purée. Rub the butter or margarine into the flour and baking powder until the mixture resembles breadcrumbs. Stir in the rhubarb, dates, egg and milk and blend together well. Spoon into a greased and lined 900 g/2 lb loaf tin (pan) and bake in a preheated oven at 190°C/375°F/gas mark 5 for 1 hour until firm to the touch.

Rice Bread

Makes one 900 g/2 lb loaf

75 g/3 oz/1/3 cup arborio or other medium-grain rice

500 ml/17 fl oz/2½ cups lukewarm water

15 g/½ oz fresh yeast or 20 ml/4 tsp dried yeast

30 ml/2 tbsp warm water

550 g/1¼ lb/6 cups strong plain (bread) flour

15 ml/1 tbsp salt

Put the rice and half the lukewarm water in a pan, bring to the boil, cover, and simmer very gently for about 25 minutes until the rice has absorbed all the liquid and bubble holes appear on the surface.

Meanwhile, mix the yeast with the warm water. When the rice is cooked, stir in the flour, salt, yeast mixture and the remaining lukewarm water and mix to a wet dough. Cover with oiled clingfilm (plastic wrap) and leave in a warm place for about 1 hour until doubled in size.

Knead the dough on a floured surface, then shape into a greased 900 g/2 lb loaf tin (pan). Cover with oiled clingfilm and leave in a warm place until the dough rises above the top of the tin. Bake in a preheated oven at 230°C/450°F/gas mark 8 for 15 minutes, then reduce the oven temperature to 200°C/400°F/gas mark 6 and bake for a further 15 minutes. Turn out of the tin and return to the oven for a further 15 minutes until crisp and brown.

Rice and Nut Tea Bread

Makes two 900 g/2 lb loaves

100 g/4 oz/½ cup long-grain rice

300 ml/½ pt/1¼ cups orange juice

400 g/14 oz/1¾ cups caster (superfine) sugar

2 eggs, beaten

50 g/2 oz/¼ cup butter or margarine, melted

Grated rind and juice of 1 orange

225 g/8 oz/2 cups plain (all-purpose) flour

175 g/6 oz/1½ cups wholemeal (wholewheat) flour

10 ml/2 tsp baking powder

5 ml/1 tsp bicarbonate of soda (baking soda)

5 ml/1 tsp salt

50 g/2 oz/½ cup walnuts, chopped

50 g/2 oz/1/3 cup sultanas (golden raisins)

50 g/2 oz/1/3 cup icing (confectioners') sugar, sifted

Cook the rice in plenty of boiling salted water for about 15 minutes until tender, then drain, rinse in cold water and drain again. Mix together the orange juice, sugar, eggs, melted butter or margarine and all but 2.5 ml/½ tsp of the orange rind – reserve the rest and the juice for the icing (frosting). Mix together the flours, baking powder, bicarbonate of soda and salt and fold in to the sugar mixture. Fold in the rice, nuts and sultanas. Spoon the mixture into two greased 900 g/2 lb loaf tins (pans) and bake in a preheated oven at 180°C/350°F/gas mark 4 for 1 hour until a skewer inserted in the centre comes out clean. Leave to cool in the tins for 10 minutes, then turn out on to a wire rack to finish cooling.

Blend the icing sugar with the reserved orange rind and enough of the juice to make a smooth, thick paste. Drizzle over the loaves and leave to set. Serve sliced and buttered.

Curly Sugar Rolls

Makes about 10

50 g/2 oz fresh yeast or 75 ml/5 tbsp dried yeast

75 g/3 oz/1/3 cup soft brown sugar

300 ml/½ pt/1¼ cups warm water

175 g/6 oz/1 cup currants

25 g/1 oz/3 tbsp stoned (pitted) dates, chopped

45 ml/3 tbsp orange juice

450 g/1 lb/4 cups wholemeal (wholewheat) flour

2.5 ml/½ tsp salt

25 g/1 oz/¼ cup milk powder (non-fat dry milk)

15 ml/1 tbsp ground mixed (apple-pie) spice

75 g/3 oz/1/3 cup butter or margarine

15 ml/1 tbsp grated orange rind

1 egg

For the filling:

30 ml/2 tbsp oil

75 g/3 oz/1/3 cup demerara sugar

For the glaze:

15 ml/1 tbsp clear honey

30 ml/2 tbsp chopped walnuts

Blend the yeast with a little of the soft brown sugar and a little of the warm water and leave in a warm place for 20 minutes until frothy. Soak the currants and dates in the orange juice. Mix together the flour, salt, milk powder and mixed spice. Rub in the butter or margarine, then stir in the orange rind and make a well in the centre. Add the yeast mixture, the remaining warm water and the egg and mix to a smooth dough. Place in an oiled bowl, cover with oiled clingfilm (plastic wrap) and leave in a warm place for 1 hour until doubled in size.

Roll out the dough on a lightly floured surface to a large rectangle. Brush with oil and sprinkle with demerara sugar. Roll up like a Swiss (jelly) roll and cut into about ten 2.5 cm/1 in slices. Arrange on a greased baking (cookie) sheet about 1 cm/½ in apart, Cover with oiled clingfilm and leave in a warm place for 40 minutes. Bake in a preheated oven at 230°C/450°F/gas mark 8 for 15 minutes until well risen. Brush with the honey, sprinkle with walnuts and leave to cool.

Selkirk Bannock

Makes one 450 g/1 lb loaf

For the dough:
225 g/8 oz/2 cups plain (all-purpose) flour

A pinch of salt

50 g/2 oz/¼ cup lard (shortening)

150 ml/¼ pt/2/3 cup milk

15 g/½ oz fresh yeast or 20 ml/4 tsp dried yeast

50 g/2 oz/¼ cup caster (superfine) sugar

100 g/4 oz/2/3 cup sultanas (golden raisins)

For the glaze:
25 g/1 oz/2 tbsp caster (superfine) sugar

30 ml/2 tbsp water

To make the dough, mix the flour and salt. Melt the lard, add the milk and bring to blood heat. Pour on to the yeast and stir in 5 ml/1 tsp of the sugar. Leave for about 20 minutes until frothy. Make a well in the centre of the flour and pour in the yeast mixture. Gradually work in the flour and knead for 5 minutes. Cover and place in a warm place for 1 hour to rise. Turn out on to a floured work surface and work in the sultanas and the remaining sugar. Shape into a large round and place on a greased baking (cookie) sheet. Cover with oiled clingfilm (plastic wrap) and leave in a warm place until doubled in size. Bake in a preheated oven at 220°C/425°F/gas mark 7 for 15 minutes. Reduce the oven temperature to 190°C/375°F/gas mark 5 and bake for a further 25 minutes. Remove from the oven. Dissolve the sugar for the glaze in the water and brush over the hot bannock.

Sultana and Carob Bread

Makes one 900 g/2 lb loaf

150 g/5 oz/1¼ cups wholemeal (wholewheat) flour

15 ml/1 tbsp baking powder

25 g/1 oz/¼ cup carob powder

50 g/2 oz/½ cup oatmeal

50 g/2 oz/¼ cup butter or margarine, softened

175 g/6 oz/1 cup sultanas (golden raisins)

2 eggs, beaten

150 ml/¼ pt/2/3 cup milk

60 ml/4 tbsp oil

Mix together the dry ingredients. Rub in the butter or margarine, then stir in the sultanas. Beat together the eggs, milk and oil, then blend into the flour mixture to make a soft dough. Shape into a greased 900 g/2 lb loaf tin (pan) and bake in a preheated oven at 180°C/350°F/gas mark 4 for 1 hour until firm to the touch.

Sultana and Orange Loaf

Makes two 450 g/1 lb loaves

For the dough:

450 g/1 lb/4 cups wholemeal (wholewheat) flour

20 ml/4 tsp baking powder

75 g/3 oz/1/3 cup soft brown sugar

5 ml/1 tsp salt

2.5 ml/½ tsp ground mace

75 g/3 oz/1/3 cup vegetable fat (shortening)

3 egg whites

300 ml/½ pt/1¼ cups milk

For the filling:

175 g/6 oz/1½ cups wholemeal (wholewheat) cake crumbs

50 g/2 oz/½ cup ground almonds

50 g/2 oz/¼ cup soft brown sugar

100 g/4 oz/2/3 cup sultanas (golden raisins)

30 ml/2 tbsp orange juice

1 egg, lightly beaten

For the glaze:

15 ml/1 tbsp honey

To make the dough, mix together the dry ingredients and rub in the fat. Mix together the egg whites and milk and blend into the mixture until you have a soft, pliable dough. Combine the filling ingredients, using just enough of the egg to make a spreading consistency. Roll out the dough on a lightly floured surface to a 20 x 30 cm/8 x 10 in rectangle. Spread the filling over all but the top 2.5 cm/1 in along the long edge. Roll up from the opposite edge, like a Swiss (jelly) roll, and moisten the plain strip of dough to seal. Moisten each end and shape the roll into a circle, sealing the ends together. With sharp scissors, make little cuts around the top for decoration. Place on a greased baking (cookie) sheet and brush with the remaining egg. Leave to rest for 15 minutes.

Bake in a preheated oven at 230°C/450°F/gas mark 8 for 25 minutes until golden brown. Brush with the honey and leave to cool.

Sultana and Sherry Bread

Makes one 900 g/2 lb loaf

225 g/8 oz/1 cup unsalted (sweet) butter or margarine, softened

225 g/8 oz/1 cup soft brown sugar

4 eggs

45 ml/3 tbsp sweet sherry

5 ml/1 tsp vanilla essence (extract)

200 g/7 oz/1¾ cups plain (all-purpose) flour

A pinch of salt

75 g/3 oz/½ cup sultanas (golden raisins)

50 g/2 oz/1/3 cup stoned (pitted) dates, chopped

50 g/2 oz/1/3 cup dried figs, diced

50 g/2 oz/½ cup chopped mixed (candied) peel

Cream together the butter or margarine and sugar until light and fluffy. Gradually add the eggs, then the sherry and vanilla essence. Mix the flour and salt with the fruit, then fold into the mixture and mix well. Spoon into a greased and floured 900 g/2 lb loaf tin (pan) and bake in a preheated oven at 180°C/350°F/gas mark 4 for 1 hour. Leave to cool in the tin for 10 minutes, then turn out on to a wire rack to finish cooling.

Cottage Tea Bread

Makes two 450 g/1 lb loaves

For the dough:

25 g/1 oz fresh yeast or 40 ml/2½ tbsp dried yeast

15 ml/1 tbsp soft brown sugar

300 ml/½ pt/1¼ cups warm water

15 ml/1 tbsp butter or margarine

450 g/1 lb/4 cups wholemeal (wholewheat) flour

15 ml/1 tbsp milk powder (non-fat dry milk)

5 ml/1 tsp ground mixed (apple-pie) spice

2.5 ml/½ tsp salt

1 egg

175 g/6 oz/1 cup currants

100 g/4 oz/2/3 cup sultanas (golden raisins)

50 g/2 oz/1/3 cup raisins

50 g/2 oz/1/3 cup chopped mixed (candied) peel

For the glaze:

15 ml/1 tbsp lemon juice

15 ml/1 tbsp water

A pinch of ground mixed (apple-pie) spice

To make the dough, blend the yeast with the sugar with a little of the warm water and leave in a warm place for 10 minutes until frothy. Rub the butter or margarine into the flour, then stir in the milk powder, mixed spice and salt and make a well in the centre. Stir in the egg, the yeast mixture and the remaining warm water and mix to a dough. Knead until smooth and elastic. Work in the currants, sultanas, raisins and mixed peel. Place in an oiled bowl, cover with oiled clingfilm (plastic wrap) and leave in warm place for 45 minutes. Shape into two greased 450 g/1 lb loaf tins (pans). Cover with oiled clingfilm and leave in a warm place for 15 minutes. Bake in a preheated oven at 220°C/425°F/gas mark 7 for 30 minutes until golden. Remove from the tin. Mix together the glaze ingredients and brush over the hot loaves, then leave to cool.

Tea Cakes

Makes 6

15 g/½ oz fresh yeast or 20 ml/4 tsp dried yeast

300 ml/½ pt/1¼ cups warm milk

25 g/1 oz/2 tbsp caster (superfine) sugar

25 g/1 oz/2 tbsp butter or margarine

450 g/1 lb/4 cups plain (all-purpose) flour

5 ml/1 tsp salt

50 g/2 oz/1/3 cup sultanas (golden raisins)

Blend the yeast with the warm milk and a little of the sugar and leave in a warm place until frothy. Rub the butter or margarine into the flour and salt, then stir in the remaining sugar and the raisins. Stir in the yeast mixture and mix to a soft dough. Turn out on to a lightly floured surface and knead until smooth. Place in an oiled bowl, cover with oiled clingfilm (plastic wrap) and leave in a warm place until doubled in size. Knead the dough again, then divide into six pieces and roll each one into a ball. Flatten slightly on a greased baking (cookie) sheet, Cover with oiled clingfilm and leave in a warm place again until doubled in size. Bake in a preheated oven at 200°C/400°F/gas mark 6 for 20 minutes.

Walnut Loaf

Makes one 900 g/2 lb loaf

350 g/12 oz/3 cups plain (all-purpose) flour

15 ml/1 tbsp baking powder

225 g/8 oz/1 cup soft brown sugar

5 ml/1 tsp salt

1 egg, lightly beaten

50 g/2 oz/¼ cup lard (shortening), melted

375 ml/13 fl oz/1½ cups milk

5 ml/1 tsp vanilla essence (extract)

175 g/6 oz/1½ cups walnuts, chopped

Mix together the flour, baking powder, sugar and salt and make a well in the centre. Stir in the egg, lard, milk and vanilla essence, then stir in the walnuts. Spoon into a greased 900 g/2 lb loaf tin (pan) and bake in a preheated oven at 180°C/350°F/gas mark 4 for about 1¼ hours until well risen and golden brown.

Walnut and Sugar Layer Loaf

Makes one 900 g/2 lb loaf

For the batter:

350 g/12 oz/3 cups plain (all-purpose) flour

15 ml/1 tbsp baking powder

225 g/8 oz/1 cup soft brown sugar

5 ml/1 tsp salt

1 egg, lightly beaten

50 g/2 oz/¼ cup lard (shortening), melted

375 ml/13 fl oz/1½ cups milk

5 ml/1 tsp vanilla essence (extract)

175 g/6 oz/1½ cups walnuts, chopped

For the filling:

15 ml/1 tbsp plain (all-purpose) flour

50 g/2 oz/¼ cup soft brown sugar

5 ml/1 tsp ground cinnamon

15 ml/1 tbsp butter, melted

To make the batter, mix together the flour, baking powder, sugar and salt and make a well in the centre. Stir in the egg, lard, milk and vanilla essence, then stir in the walnuts. Spoon half the mixture into a greased 900 g/2 lb loaf tin (pan). Mix together the filling ingredients and spoon over the batter. Spoon over the remaining batter and bake in a preheated oven at 180°C/350°F/gas mark 4 for about 1¼ hours until well risen and golden brown.

Walnut and Orange Loaf

Makes one 900 g/2 lb loaf

350 g/12 oz/3 cups plain (all-purpose) flour

15 ml/1 tbsp baking powder

225 g/8 oz/1 cup soft brown sugar

5 ml/1 tsp salt

1 egg, lightly beaten

5 ml/1 tsp grated orange rind

50 g/2 oz/¼ cup lard (shortening), melted

375 ml/13 fl oz/1½ cups milk

5 ml/1 tsp vanilla essence (extract)

175 g/6 oz/1½ cups walnuts, chopped

50 g/2 oz/1/3 cup chopped mixed (candied) peel

Mix together the flour, baking powder, sugar and salt and make a well in the centre. Stir in the egg, orange rind, lard, milk and vanilla essence, then stir in the walnuts and mixed peel. Spoon into a greased 900 g/2 lb loaf tin (pan) and bake in a preheated oven at 180°C/350°F/gas mark 4 for about 1¼ hours until well risen and golden brown.

Asparagus Loaf

Makes one 900 g/2 lb loaf

50 g/2 oz/¼ cup butter or margarine

2 shallots, finely grated

100 g/4 oz wholemeal bread, diced

10 ml/2 tsp chopped fresh parsley

1.5 ml/¼ tsp salt

450 g/1 lb asparagus

2 eggs, lightly beaten

450 ml/¾ pt/2 cups hot milk

Melt the butter or margarine and fry (sauté) the shallots, bread, parsley and salt until lightly browned. Remove from the heat and place in a bowl. Trim the tough ends off the asparagus and cut the stems into 2.5 cm/1 in lengths and add to the bowl. Blend together the eggs and milk, then mix into the remaining ingredients. Spoon into a greased 900 g/2 lb loaf tin (pan) and press down lightly. Bake in a preheated oven at 190°C/375°F/gas mark 5 for 30 minutes until firm to the touch.